compass

exploring **Christian faith** together

The **Methodist** Church

Contents

Introduction

Welcome to *Compass*. This short course is intended to give a bearing on issues about the Christian faith for those wishing to explore its meaning. Like any compass, it relates to a particular map and the one intended is discipleship in the Methodist Church. We look not just at the particular issues of the Church today, but also to the distant hills and valleys of Methodist heritage which have shaped our present understanding.

Compass is intended to give you an opportunity to explore the significant aspects of Christian faith and to anchor them in your experience of life. At all points there is a chance to discuss, reflect and question in the context of a small group.

In that sense *Compass* is a process of learning, an opportunity for sharing and a vehicle for deepening our faith and spiritual insight into the way of Jesus. It is intended as a guide on the journey of exploring discipleship. It ought to come with a health warning, for the teaching of Jesus is subversive; it challenges contemporary assumptions and overturns social norms but the effect is to transform people and communities. So read with eagerness, share with openness, listen with care and may God bless you as you engage on this journey.

The Compass Team

Those involved in writing and editing *Compass* have been Jenny Ellis, Bev Hollings, Roger Johnson, Ken Kingston, Piers Lane, Howard Mellor, Viv Morrissey, Nick Moxon and Martin Wellings, with helpful advice from the Faith and Order Committee.

Some ground rules

Exploring and sharing ideas is much safer and the group is able to go 'deeper' with each other if some ground rules have been agreed. Here are some common ground rules – try them out and see if there are any other suggestions.

- The group will start and finish on time.
- Everyone is committed to attending every session unless they are ill or genuinely prevented from meeting.
- We will listen carefully to each other. And we will think about what others are trying to say, and what God may be saying to us through them.
- We will watch out for one another and invite others to speak rather than hog the floor.
- We will respect the fact that someone else may express things differently from how we would express them. God is fine with this, so we will resist the temptation to 'fix' their view or them.
- Disagreement and searching questions are acceptable, when expressed sensitively and with respect.
- Personal information shared within the group is confidential and should not be passed on without permission.
- Other (write in below…)

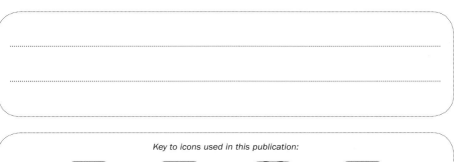

Key to icons used in this publication:

Discuss

Read

Reflect

Activity

Session 1: Glimpses of God

Opening prayer

Mysterious God,
we have heard many things about you
and wonder what it might be like to know
*   you for ourselves.*
Do you really know and love us?
What does forgiveness and a new
*   beginning look like in our lives?*
Can we trust you to help us find our
*   special purpose and live courageously?*
Help us discover more of you for
*   ourselves.*
Hear our prayer. Amen.

Introduction

What do you make of these statements?

- There is a God-shaped gap in the life of every person.
- Life is more than we can see or touch.
- I don't need God, even if some people find the notion helpful.
- I have met some people who say that God is very real to them.
- There is something in this Christianity but I am not sure how it relates to me.
- I am just looking.

 1. Choose one which speaks to you and say why.

Picturing God

A young lad was sitting in school painting a picture. His teacher asked him, "What are you painting?" "I'm painting a picture of God," he replied. "But no one has ever seen God so we don't know what God looks like," said the teacher. "They soon will when I've finished this," replied the boy.

1

2. How do you picture God? Try drawing a picture if that helps.

3. From the things you have heard about God what words, colour, or image best depict these views?

Encountering the word

The Bible shows people experiencing God in many different ways, just like we do. Here are two encounters that people had with God.

Holy God

In this passage, one of the significant prophets of the Old Testament, Isaiah, has a dramatic vision of God in the temple.

Isaiah 6:1-3

In the year that King Uzziah died, I saw the Lord sitting on a throne, high and lofty; and the hem of his robe filled the temple. Seraphs were in attendance above him; each had six wings: with two they covered their faces, and with two they covered their feet, and with two they flew. And one called to another and said: "Holy, holy, holy is the Lord of hosts; the whole earth is full of his glory."

4. What do you think it means to say God is holy? How do you feel about this image of God?

God of extravagant mercy

This is one of the best known parables of Jesus. The two main characters interact in an amazing way – the father, sometimes likened to God, and the younger son, representing a wayward people.

Luke 15:11-13

Then Jesus said, "There was a man who had two sons. The younger of them said to his father, 'Father, give me the share of the property that will belong to me.' So he divided his property between them. A few days later the younger son gathered all he had and travelled to a distant country, and there he squandered his property in dissolute living.

5. How do you think the father felt when the son said these things and left?

Luke 15:14-20

When he had spent everything, a severe famine took place throughout that country, and he began to be in need. So he went and hired himself out to one of the citizens of that country, who sent him to his fields to feed the pigs. He would gladly have filled himself with the pods that the pigs were eating; and no one gave him anything. But when he came to himself he said, 'How many of my father's hired hands have bread enough and to spare, but here I am dying of hunger! I will

2

3

4

5

get up and go to my father, and I will say to him, "Father, I have sinned against heaven and before you; I am no longer worthy to be called your son; treat me like one of your hired hands."' So he set off and went to his father.

6. What do you think the father was doing/feeling at this time?

Luke 15:20-24
But while he was still far off, his father saw him and was filled with compassion; he ran and put his arms around him and kissed him. Then the son said to him, 'Father, I have sinned against heaven and before you; I am no longer worthy to be called your son.' But the father said to his slaves, 'Quickly, bring out a robe – the best one – and put it on him; put a ring on his finger and sandals on his feet. And get the fatted calf and kill it, and let us eat and celebrate; for this son of mine was dead and is alive again; he was lost and is found!' And they began to celebrate.

7. What do you think this experience would do for the younger son?

Luke 15:25-32
Now his elder son was in the field; and when he came and approached the house, he heard music and dancing. He called one of the slaves and asked what was going on. He replied, 'Your brother has come, and your father has killed the fatted calf, because he has got him back safe and sound.' Then he became angry and refused to go in. His father came out and began to plead with him. But he answered his father, 'Listen! For all these years I have been working like a slave for you, and I have never disobeyed your command; yet you have never given me even a young goat so that I might celebrate with my friends. But when this son of yours came back, who has devoured your property with prostitutes, you killed the fatted calf for him!' Then the father said to him, 'Son, you are always with me, and all that is mine is yours. But we had to celebrate and rejoice, because this brother of yours was dead and has come to life; he was lost and has been found.'"

8a. If you were the older son how would you respond in the story?

8b. What does the response of the father say about the nature of God?

8c. What continuing questions do you have?

6

7

8

a

b

c

The Psalms

The Psalms are a collection of responses to God emerging out of the experience of the writers. They were hymns which were sung in the temple and represented the many ways people expressed their thoughts, emotions and desires to God.

Here is a sample of them:

Psalm 139:1-3, 13-15 (God knows us from the beginning)

O Lord, you have searched me and known me.
You know when I sit down and when I rise up;
you discern my thoughts from far away.
You search out my path and my lying down,
and are acquainted with all my ways. ...

For it was you who formed my inward parts;
you knit me together in my mother's womb.
I praise you, for I am fearfully and wonderfully made.
Wonderful are your works; that I know very well.
My frame was not hidden from you,
when I was being made in secret,
intricately woven in the depths of the earth.

Psalm 51:1-2, 10-12 (A cry for forgiveness)

Have mercy on me, O God,
according to your steadfast love;
according to your abundant mercy
blot out my transgressions.
Wash me thoroughly from my iniquity,
and cleanse me from my sin. ...

Create in me a clean heart, O God,
and put a new and right spirit within me.
Do not cast me away from your presence,
and do not take your holy spirit from me.

Restore to me the joy of your salvation,
and sustain in me a willing spirit.

Psalm 82:1-4, 8 (God's justice is called for)

God has taken his place in the divine council;
in the midst of the gods he holds judgement:
"How long will you judge unjustly
and show partiality to the wicked?
Give justice to the weak and the orphan;
maintain the right of the lowly and the destitute.
Rescue the weak and the needy;
deliver them from the hand of the wicked." ...

Rise up, O God, judge the earth;
for all the nations belong to you!

Psalm 95:1-7 (An invitation to worship an awesome God)

O come, let us sing to the Lord;
let us make a joyful noise to the rock of
    our salvation!
Let us come into his presence with
    thanksgiving;
let us make a joyful noise to him with
    songs of praise!
For the Lord is a great God,
and a great King above all gods.
In his hand are the depths of the earth;
the heights of the mountains are his also.
The sea is his, for he made it,
and the dry land, which his hands have
    formed.

O come, let us worship and bow down,
let us kneel before the Lord, our Maker!
For he is our God,
and we are the people of his pasture,
and the sheep of his hand.

 Psalm 18:1-3 (A place of safety and sanctuary)

I love you, O Lord, my strength.
The Lord is my rock, my fortress, and my
    deliverer,
my God, my rock in whom I take refuge,
my shield, and the horn of my salvation,
    my stronghold.
I call upon the Lord, who is worthy to be
    praised;
so I shall be saved from my enemies.

 9. Choose one psalm and express the feeling of the writer in your own words.

OR Choose a passage which expresses your feelings towards God and share your reflections.

OR Building on the experience of the psalmist, how would you express your experience of God?

9

....
....
....
....
....
....

The Methodist emphasis

John and Charles Wesley began the movement which has become Methodism. John was its leader, but Charles wrote many hymns and captured the way the early Methodists expressed their thoughts about God and God's transforming love for us. It was through the singing of Charles Wesley's hymns that the early Methodists learned their theology and their beliefs about God. Here is one of the best known:

Love divine, all loves excelling,
joy of heaven to earth come down,
fix in us thy humble dwelling,
all thy faithful mercies crown.
Jesu, thou art all compassion,
pure, unbounded love thou art;
visit us with thy salvation,
enter every trembling heart.

Come, almighty to deliver,
let us all thy life receive;
suddenly return, and never,
never more thy temples leave.
Thee we would be always blessing,
serve thee as thy hosts above,
pray, and praise thee, without ceasing,
glory in thy perfect love.

Finish then thy new creation,
pure and spotless let us be;
let us see thy great salvation,
perfectly restored in thee:
changed from glory into glory,

till in heaven we take our place,
till we cast our crowns before thee,
lost in wonder, love, and praise!

Charles Wesley (1707-1788) (Singing the Faith 503)

 10a. If you had to pick out a favourite phrase from this hymn to keep in your wallet or purse, or to place on a book mark, which would it be? Why?

10b. How would you describe the God this hymn speaks about?

10c. What does the hymn tell you about a Methodist understanding of our response to God?

The thoughts of the Scriptures are often in the hymns and prayers used in our Methodist services. In Baptism services there is a passage which declares that God not only knows us but loves us from the very beginning before ever we could know about it.

… for you Jesus Christ came into the world;
for you he lived and showed God's love;
for you he suffered death on the Cross;
for you he triumphed over death,
rising to newness of life;
for you he prays at God's right hand:
all this for you,
before you could know anything of it.
In your Baptism,

the word of Scripture is fulfilled:
"We love, because God first loved us."

Methodist Worship Book, pp.92-93

How do you react to such a promise?

What does this suggest to you about how Methodists believe God relates to each one of us?

Prayer reflection: thanksgiving

As we come to the end of the session we have an opportunity to give thanks to God, using a very simple but effective prayer. You will be given the image of a flower copied onto paper. Cut out the flower, and in its centre write down the things you wish to give thanks for. Colour the petals reflecting on all God has created and provided. Then fold the petals inwards along the dotted line.

Place the flower on a tray or bowl of water, or if you are meeting in the church and there is a large enough font available, use that. Place the folded flowers in the water, with one person perhaps saying a general prayer of thanksgiving, and watch the prayers open up before God.

10

a ....

....

....

b ....

....

....

c ....

....

....

A Bible passage to look at this week

Read Psalm 34:1-3 as the way we respond to God.

I will bless the Lord at all times;
his praise shall continually be in my mouth.
My soul makes its boast in the Lord;
let the humble hear and be glad.
O magnify the Lord with me,
and let us exalt his name together.

Prayer to use this week

Jesus, open my eyes to your presence,
open my ears to your word,
open my heart to your love.
Grant me grace to follow you,
wisdom to discern the way
and strength in times of challenge.
Help me to trust you
and give myself to you,
so that I may follow in your ways
and be your true disciple. Amen.

To think about: Methodist beginnings

At its heart Methodism believes that we cannot simply know God by reasoning alone; we also need to experience God in a personal way. The key founders of Methodism were John and Charles Wesley. Brought up in the parsonage at Epworth in Lincolnshire, where their father was the Anglican rector, they were raised in a tradition of disciplined spirituality. At Oxford University in the 1720s they continued to be 'methodical' in living out their Christian faith, and they progressed to ordination in the Church of England.

For the Wesley brothers, the year 1738 was a pivotal moment. They both experienced the grace and love of God in a life-transforming way. In 1735 John and Charles had sailed to America, hoping to find a pure Christian society in the New World. They were sadly disappointed: Charles Wesley fell ill and came home within a year, while John quarrelled with the colonists and left under a cloud at the end of 1737. Reflecting later on the experience, John Wesley highlighted an encounter on board ship with a group of Moravian Christians who, in the midst of a fierce storm, calmly worshipped God together. He described the conversation with their leader in his journal:

Charles and John Wesley: detail from stained glass window
Wesley Memorial Church, Epworth © TMCP.

"Were you not afraid?" He answered, "I thank God, no." I asked, "But were not your women and children afraid?" He replied mildly, "No; our women and children are not afraid to die."

It was at this point that John Wesley realised that his faith was sadly lacking; it was in his head but not in his heart. Back in London, in May 1738, Wesley went somewhat reluctantly to a Moravian gathering in Aldersgate Street. He described his experience of God like this:

I felt my heart strangely warmed. I felt I did trust in Christ, Christ alone, for salvation; and an assurance was given me that he had taken away my sins, even mine, and saved me from the law of sin and death.

Underpinning this personal experience and assurance of God's love was a conviction of the priority of God's grace. John Wesley turned from being absorbed about his own spiritual condition into an ardent evangelist. He rediscovered the message of the apostle Paul and of the reformers that people are put right with God by grace, and not by good works, respectability or even religious behaviour. This was a revolutionary and controversial message in the 1730s.

Such a view of God results in an assurance that we are children of God.

Paul writes this in Romans 8:15-16:

For you did not receive a spirit of slavery to fall back into fear, but you have received a spirit of adoption. When we cry, "Abba! Father!" it is that very Spirit bearing witness with our spirit that we are children of God.

What Paul describes here is similar to what John Wesley experienced on 24 May 1738 in the Aldersgate Street meeting. Salvation became a personal reality.

 11. What do you find significant in Wesley's experience?

12. How has this first session helped you reflect on your, and other people's, experience of God?

11

12

Session 2: Meeting Jesus today

Opening prayer

Loving God,
we sometimes sense your presence,
then find words inadequate.
You are awesome, uncontainable,
yet intimate, closer than our breath.
Help us – to let you find us, to stop hiding.
We have heard much about your Son,
and now, we want to meet him ourselves.
When he calls us by name,
how do we hear that call?
How do we live courageously
and with love?
Show us what it means to follow Jesus
today.
Hear our prayer. Amen.

Welcome

Briefly share insights and reflections as a result of the previous session and your reading since we last met.

 In front of you there are a number of images of Jesus from around the world. Choose one that strikes you, or speaks to you. Share with others why you chose it.

 What other images of Jesus have you seen which you have found helpful or unhelpful? Why?

Encountering the word

Here are two passages about people who met Jesus. Picture yourself as being part of the story, and choose one of the roles listed below.

As the passage is read, where are you standing, what do you see and hear? What are your reactions or responses?

Zacchaeus
Possible roles are:
- Zacchaeus
- Jesus
- one of the crowd
- Zacchaeus' cook or a servant
- a fellow tax collector.

 Luke 19:1-10
[Jesus] entered Jericho and was passing through it. A man was there named Zacchaeus; he was a chief tax collector and was rich. He was trying to see who Jesus was, but on account of the crowd he could not, because he was short in stature. So he ran ahead and climbed a sycamore tree to see him, because he was going to pass that way. When Jesus came

to the place, he looked up and said to him, *"Zacchaeus, hurry and come down; for I must stay at your house today."* So he hurried down and was happy to welcome him. All who saw it began to grumble and said, *"He has gone to be the guest of one who is a sinner."* Zacchaeus stood there and said to the Lord, *"Look, half of my possessions, Lord, I will give to the poor; and if I have defrauded anyone of anything, I will pay back four times as much."* Then Jesus said to him, *"Today salvation has come to this house, because he too is a son of Abraham. For the Son of Man came to seek out and to save the lost."*

A bit of background information

- Zacchaeus was a man on the make! Jericho was an important oasis city on the route from Egypt to Jerusalem. It was therefore a lucrative place to be the chief tax collector.
- The chief tax collector would franchise the collecting to others and charge for the privilege, so the collectors would have to charge extra to make their own living and to fund their chief (Zacchaeus).
- Zacchaeus was willing to sacrifice his dignity (by climbing a tree) as well as cope with the hostility of the crowd in order to see Jesus.
- Zacchaeus was regarded as a sinner or an outcast, for two reasons. First he

was working for and with the Romans, which meant he was constantly polluted by Gentiles (non-Jews) and was a traitor. Secondly because he was, in effect, stealing from his fellow Jews, he was stereotyped by society, a traitor shunned and avoided.

- Jesus' self-invitation to stay with Zacchaeus was extraordinary. To eat and stay with someone was to associate with them and become polluted by their sin. No self-respecting rabbi (Jewish teacher of the law) would contemplate such a compromising step. Jesus was not technically a rabbi but was perceived to fit into that pattern as he had disciples and moved around teaching about God.

 1. As you listened to the passage from the point of view of one of the characters, what did you see and hear? What were your reactions or responses?

2. When the incident is over, and supposing you came back a month later, in the same role, what if anything do you think would have changed?

1

2

The woman who reached out to Jesus

Possible roles are:

- the woman
- a disciple
- one of the bustling crowd
- Jesus.

Mark 5:25-34

Now there was a woman who had been suffering from haemorrhages for twelve years. She had endured much under many physicians, and had spent all that she had; and she was no better, but rather grew worse. She had heard about Jesus, and came up behind him in the crowd and touched his cloak, for she said, "If I but touch his clothes, I will be made well." Immediately her haemorrhage stopped; and she felt in her body that she was healed of her disease. Immediately aware that power had gone forth from him, Jesus turned about in the crowd and said, "Who touched my clothes?" And his disciples said to him, "You see the crowd pressing in on you; how can you say, 'Who touched me?'" He looked all round to see who had done it. But the woman, knowing what had happened to her, came in fear and trembling, fell down before him, and told him the whole truth. He said to her, "Daughter, your faith has made you well; go in peace, and be healed of your disease."

A bit of background information

- Jesus had an important appointment, rushing to help the daughter of Jairus, one of the leaders of the synagogue (see Mark 5:22-23, 35-43). But to Jesus this woman was just as important.

- There was a crowd of excited people crushing into the narrow streets of this lakeside town.

- Suddenly Jesus stopped and asked, "Who touched me?" Imagine the disciples' surprise, in this crowded narrow street with people pushing and shoving – what a silly thing to say!

- The woman had intended to be unnoticed. She feared the insults from people who despised her condition, which made her unclean and an outcast.

- Jesus focused the spotlight on her. The Bible does not say anything here, but one can imagine Jesus reaching out, taking hold of her hand and lifting her to stand upright in the presence of all the people. He gives her dignity and status which for so many years had been denied her. She is made well, literally 'made whole'.

- The healing was in body, mind and spirit. She was given dignity in the community and while others rushed off to Jairus' house she undoubtedly went and showed herself to the priest who would pronounce her healed and able to enter society again.

 3. As you listened to the passage from the point of view of one of the characters, what do you see and hear? What are your reactions or responses?

4. When the incident is over, and supposing you came back a month later, in the same role, what if anything do you think would have changed?

What do we know about Jesus?

 5a. What do you know about the story of Jesus?

5b. What questions do you have about this story of Jesus?

5c. What parts of the story of Jesus do you want to know more about?

5d. What are the surprising things about Jesus?

The Methodist emphasis

Methodism started in a time of revival. Those who write about this time note the activism of the early Methodists as well as the preaching of the Cross, the commitment to read the Scriptures (the Bible) and the call for people to know salvation.

3

4

5

a

b

c

d

- Early Methodists believed that Christians are called to be the hands and feet of Jesus.
- Changed by knowing Jesus, they felt compelled to join in God's work by making a positive difference in the world.
- Methodism's heritage is one of social transformation – establishing trade unions, visiting prisoners, helping the poor by feeding, clothing and even lending them money, forming schools, orphanages, and opening church buildings to people in need.
- Methodists became known and trusted as people of transformed character. In his book about John Wesley, *A brand from the burning*, Roy Hattersley (the Labour politician and author) tells the story about a Lancashire mill owner who would only employ Methodists as foremen. The mill owner was not a Christian but he recognised that the Methodists were honest, fair, hardworking and trusted by colleagues.
- The last letter John Wesley ever wrote was to William Wilberforce MP to encourage him to continue campaigning against the slave trade.

6. What do you think Christians mean by being a 'transformed character'?

Priorities for the Methodist Church

More recently the Methodist Conference has defined the priorities for the Church today. As you read the priorities which follow, what are your responses to the following questions?

7a. What is your response to these as a set of priorities for the Church today?

7b. Where do you see them in action?

7c. What is the challenge for your life?

In partnership with others wherever possible, the Methodist Church will concentrate its prayers, resources, imagination and commitments on this priority:

To proclaim and affirm its conviction of God's love in Christ, for us and for all the world; and renew confidence in God's presence and action in the world and in the Church.

As ways towards realising this priority, the Methodist Church will give particular attention to the following:

- *underpinning everything we do with God-centred worship and prayer*
- *supporting community development and action for justice, especially among the most deprived and poor – in Britain and worldwide*

6

7

a

b

c

- *developing confidence in evangelism and in the capacity to speak of God and faith in ways that make sense to all involved*
- *encouraging fresh ways of being Church*
- *nurturing a culture in the Church which is people-centred and flexible.*

Priorities for the Methodist Church, agreed at the Methodist Conference 2004

Prayer reflection: this time tomorrow

What are the major things you will be doing in the coming week. Who will you be with?

 How may you be able to be the hands and feet of Jesus in the situations in which you will find yourself?

After a moment of silence say this prayer together:

Christ be with me, Christ within me,
Christ behind me, Christ before me,
Christ beside me, Christ to win me,
Christ to comfort and restore me,
Christ beneath me, Christ above me,
Christ in quiet, Christ in danger,
Christ in hearts of all that love me,
Christ in mouth of friend and stranger.

St Patrick (c 372-466)

And finally …

 8. Methodists suggest that the essence of being a Christian is a God-inspired person being transformed into a Christ-like person in character and action. How do you respond to this?

A Bible passage to look at this week

Let the same mind be in you that was in
*   Christ Jesus,*
who, though he was in the form of God,
did not regard equality with God
as something to be exploited,
but emptied himself,
taking the form of a slave,
being born in human likeness.
And being found in human form,
he humbled himself
and became obedient to the point of death
– even death on a cross.

Therefore God also highly exalted him
and gave him the name
that is above every name,
so that at the name of Jesus
every knee should bend,
in heaven and on earth and under the earth,
and every tongue should confess
that Jesus Christ is Lord,
to the glory of God the Father.

Philippians 2:5-11

8

....
....
....
....
....
....
....
....
....

Prayer to use this week

Use St Patrick's prayer (see page 26) each day and reflect on how your day matches the prayer.

To think about: Jesus

Jesus met and had a positive (many times a life-changing) impact on people. Today, Christians still believe that people can meet Jesus and receive that same positive and life-changing impact from him.

What do we make of Jesus?

Jesus is the centre of the Christian faith.

Who then is he?

Here is the story in brief:

A Palestinian carpenter born in obscurity, a refugee who in early life seems to have taken responsibility in his family? One day he kissed his mother goodbye and dropped the latch on his workshop and began a ministry of preaching, healing and teaching. He called 12 disciples and a wider circle of women and men to share in that ministry. He began to speak of why he had really come and ultimately that took him to a city-wide welcome in Jerusalem. There he shared in a meal with his disciples, and spoke of bread and wine as symbols of his dying love for all people. Then in a garden, under cover of darkness, he was arrested, tried on false charges, stripped, whipped and made to carry his own cross beam out of the city to a hill called Golgotha. There he was crucified with two thieves on the Friday that we call Good. Friends took him down and laid him in a tomb, but early on the Sunday women found he had risen. Astonished, they ran to tell incredulous disciples. Slowly it dawned on them that Jesus was alive, and he did appear to them on a number of occasions. Finally he instructed them to make disciples wherever they went, and to baptize and pass on his teaching. They were to receive power to do this when the promised Holy Spirit came. The Holy Spirit did come on the feast of Pentecost and then the real fun started!

What Jesus did for the disciples, he does for us: the Holy Spirit came for them and now empowers us as followers of Jesus to live and work for him.

What historical evidence is there about Jesus life?

There are the Gospel records which we can read (Matthew, Mark, Luke and John) but there is also much other evidence. Roman Emperors were proud, so they appointed historians and some of their work survives.

They do not view Christianity or Jesus with anything but contempt. One of them, Suetonius, says, "Punishment by Nero was inflicted on the Christians, a class of men given to a new and mischievous superstition" (*Lives of the Caesars,* 26.2). Another, called Tacitus, writes, "Christus, the founder of the name, was put to death by Pontius Pilate, procurator of Judea in the reign of Tiberius: but the pernicious superstition, repressed for a time broke out again, not only through Judea, where the mischief originated, but through the city of Rome also" (*Annals,* XV.44).

Of course the real question about Christianity is not one of history, but of faith. History shows Jesus existed, but it is faith which says he is Lord and Saviour. There is much in the New Testament which indicates that Jesus is both human and divine.

How did Jesus describe himself?

It seems curious at first, but the term he uses is 'Son of Man'. Why do that? If Jesus had proclaimed himself as Messiah then the Jews would have expected him to overthrow the Roman invaders and restore Israel as a strong nation. But Jesus comes to do something bigger than that: to proclaim good news of the kingdom of God for all humankind.

The term 'Son of Man' is a clumsy phrase in Hebrew, Greek and English! It occurs in the Old Testament where it often means simply 'man'. However in the later books, and most noticeably in Daniel 7:13-14, the Son of Man is seen as a pre-existent heavenly figure. Although used in this way between the Old and New Testaments (about 250 years), in Jesus' day the term was not widely used. Jesus takes the term 'Son of Man' and fills it with new meaning.

Jesus emphasised that the Son of Man came as a human being, eating and drinking (Matthew 11:19; Luke 7:34), and that he has a humiliated existence (Matthew 8:20; Luke 9:58). This focuses on the earthly Son of Man, but there is more.

The exchange with the disciples at Caesarea Philippi (Mark 8:27-33) marks a turning point in Jesus' self-disclosure to his disciples. Until then he has only spoken of himself as an earthly Son of Man. But now he announces that the Son of Man must suffer and die, a thought foreign to all the Jewish literature and distasteful to Peter. Here is a suffering Son of Man (see also Mark 10:45).

The teaching of Jesus about himself does not end there, for to the novel idea of a Son of Man that lives as a human being and suffers and dies, Jesus adds the more usual theme that the Son of Man will come in glory. At Jesus'

sham trial he answers the high priest Caiaphas' question as to whether he was the Messiah, the Son of God, in the affirmative (Matthew 26:64; Mark 14:62). Jesus immediately interprets what he means and suggests that in effect the roles would be reversed. The day will come when they, Jesus' judges, would stand before his tribunal and he, the heavenly Son of Man, would be the judge.

Jesus did not use the term 'Messiah' of himself because of its overtones in popular thought where a Messiah was expected to be the conquering king. He comes in peace to show what God is really like and to establish peace, justice and joy of God's way for us to live as individuals and together as a society.

What did the disciples say?
Jesus, by his words and actions, is identified as the Son of God (or Messiah) to the disciples (Mark 8:29). He has the essential relationship with the Father that can bring a new and full revelation of God (Matthew 11:27; Hebrews 1:1-4).

Consider the words of the disciple Thomas when he addresses the risen Christ as "my Lord and my God" (John 20:28). Thomas comes to the same conclusion as the other disciples but after a struggle of faith. He has followed Jesus willingly and now recognises Jesus as God the Son.

What did Jesus' opponents say?

What is intriguing is the response of Jesus' opponents. In John 5:16-18 the Jewish leaders are certain that Jesus makes himself equal with God. Similarly in Mark 2:1-12, the scribes are scandalised that Jesus says he can forgive sins. Jesus' answer is of the most convincing kind.

The early Church's quest to describe Jesus

The discussion about the nature of Jesus as fully human and fully divine is nothing new. There was one Church Council (at Nicaea in AD325) that lasted for months with this as the most important agenda item! Some in the Church were saying that the Son may be said to be like the Father or similar to the Father, but not of the same nature or essence as the Father. However the biblical witness is that Jesus is described as 'only begotten' (John 1:14; 3:16, 18; 1 John 4:9), and here we meet the problem of language. 'Begotten' sounds like a child of a parent. However the word 'begotten' comes from *genos* meaning kind or essence rather than *gennao* which means 'beget'. In other words 'begotten' in John describes the closeness of the relationship between the Father and the Son, meaning Jesus is of the same essence as the Father. Thus in the Nicene Creed that we read in Holy Communion services we affirm that Christ was "begotten, not made".

 9. How has this helped your understanding of Jesus?

9

Session 3: The difference Jesus makes

Opening prayer

Life-giving God,
we know that Jesus told amazing stories,
and profoundly changed people he met
when he walked on the earth.
We are intrigued and inspired by him.
But why did he have to die?
So young, such a terrible waste,
which seems to make no sense.
Help us to enter the mystery
of what changed in his death
and what changes for us,
as we learn about the one
who conquered death.
Hear our prayer. Amen.

Welcome

Briefly describe the insights and questions about the life of Jesus which have been uppermost in your mind since we last met.

Introduction

In this session we are looking at a tough story. It is about the scandal of a popular hero tricked by the authorities, tried on fabricated charges and given a cruel death. It is the Easter story which in popular imagery we have abandoned in favour of bunnies, chocolate and chicks.

The story of Holy Week

Jesus had been on the way to Jerusalem for some time. His disciples tried but did not really understand his main purpose in coming. On the day we call Palm Sunday Jesus came with his disciples from Bethany and Bethphage, and, mounting a donkey, rode into the city as the crowd welcomed him. The city authorities tried to catch him out with questions which might show he offended the Roman or the religious authorities, so that they would have an excuse to arrest him.

On the Thursday Jesus has a meal with his disciples and washes their feet. After the meal they share bread and wine. Jesus goes, as he often did, to the olive grove at Gethsemane, where he prays. Here, under cover of darkness, Judas leads the soldiers to find him.

Jesus is quickly brought before three courts: the Jewish leaders', Herod's and Pilate's. Witnesses are brought, but no accusation seems without question. Finally, before a morning crowd, Pilate offers to release a prisoner and suggests

Jesus. But the crowd shout "Crucify him!" Pilate agrees unwillingly and washes his hands of the situation. Jesus is, at Pilate's orders, whipped and stripped, tied to the cross beam he must carry through Jerusalem, and with two others is marched stumbling to the hill outside the city called Golgotha. There he is crucified with two criminals. The disciples flee, his opponents jeer, and soldiers throw dice for his clothes. Jesus cries out and dies. His mother Mary and other women are there. The disciple John is with them. Many others witness this event.

The women and a rich friend, Joseph, take down his body and place it in a tomb, wrapped carefully. Nothing happens on the Saturday, the Sabbath. But early on the Sunday morning the women come to place spices and herbs with the body. In the mist they see someone they assume to be the gardener. The resonance of his voice tells them this is Jesus – the tomb is empty. He is not there! Jesus appears to the women first, then the disciples. Amazing, He is risen! These three words change their world.

 Looking at the focus point, with its cross and hill, imagine this is the scene outside Jerusalem. There are cards which identify the people we know were there. Where do you think they were? Are they near the cross or far away? Are they closing in or backing off? Place the names in the scene and talk together about the things we know they said.

 From what you know of the Easter story:

1. What character would you be?

2. Where would you be standing? What would you be feeling?

3. If you had something to say what would it be?

 Share together about the way the scene changes as the women discover the empty tomb on Easter Day.

Houston, we have a problem!

Why does Jesus need to make a difference?

In the face of God's extravagant generosity, people have rebelled against God's best for us. This means all people everywhere, including those of us who write or read this material. There does seem to be a significant problem for humankind.

1

2

3

Using the newspapers from this week, find some current news stories.

- ***What is the overall impression they give about humankind?***
- ***If this was the only window you had on the way people act towards others, what would you conclude?***
- ***How would you describe people's normal attitude, behaviour, relationships and values?***
- ***Think about the news stories you have identified. In a sophisticated world why are we still torn apart by war, poverty, racial conflict and exploitation?***

Encounter the word

Consider these texts from the Bible, all of which describe humankind.

For there is no distinction, since all have sinned and fall short of the glory of God. Romans 3:22-23

For the wages of sin is death, but the free gift of God is eternal life in Christ Jesus our Lord. Romans 6:23

I came that they may have life, and have it abundantly. John 10:10

Teacher … what must I do to inherit eternal life?… You shall love the Lord your God with all your heart, and with all your soul, and with all your mind; and your neighbour as yourself.

Luke 10:25,27

So if anyone is in Christ, there is a new creation: everything old has passed away; see, everything has become new! All this is from God, who reconciled us to himself through Christ, and has given us the ministry of reconciliation; **that is, in Christ God was reconciling the world to himself,** *not counting their trespasses against them, and entrusting the message of reconciliation to us.*

2 Corinthians 5:17-19

 Think of a situation, from the news or your experience, where you know people need to be reconciled.

4. What makes this reconciliation so necessary?

5. Why do we need to be reconciled to God?

4

5

Images of the difference Jesus makes

When we think about the difference Jesus makes through the Cross and Resurrection, we are speaking of the most incredible mystery. This is the glorious mystery that God in Christ dies for us, and in his person takes on all the suffering and hurt, and pain and sin of all people in every place and for all time.

God comes to rescue and liberate us that we may be the people God wants us to be.

The writers of the New Testament used five images as they sought to convey in words what they believed to be the truth about the death and resurrection of Jesus. They were seeking to describe the difference Jesus makes for us.

6. As you read the next sections, make a note of what for you are the key words or phrases.

Practice in the temple

The image here is of the sacrificial system of the temple in which there is a sacrifice for sin. There is a word, *hilasmos*, which we find in Luke 18:13, Romans 3:25, Hebrews 2:17 and 1 John 2:2; 4:10. In more recent versions of the English Bible the word is translated using the phrase 'atoning sacrifice'.

These writers are seeking to convey that God in Christ dies on the Cross for us. His sacrifice deals with sin, once and for all. The great writer PT Forsyth put it so eloquently saying, "The atonement did not procure grace – it flowed from it." God does not love us because Christ died for us; Christ died for us because God loves us. In this sense, the death of Jesus was God's perfect gift to make a way for us.

Transactions in the market place

The word *lutroo* means 'to redeem'. It is a technical term that appears in Mark 10:45 and was used in the sense of buying back, or setting free. In the Old Testament, property, animals, persons and even a nation can be set free. 1 Timothy 2:5-6 also contains this idea of ransom.

Ransom is also about liberation. There are many images within the Bible which speak of liberation, not least Moses and the children of Israel (Exodus 12), or people Jesus dealt with such as Zacchaeus (Luke 19:1-10), or the woman at the well (John 4:7-30). Jesus is our liberator, setting us free from sin to "walk in newness of life" (Romans 6:4). By this 'ransom' the holy love of God comes to set us free from personal and structural sin; to become the very people God wants us to be.

6

....

....

....

....

....

Judgement in the law court

In the courtroom the people before the judge are found guilty, but having pronounced judgement, the judge comes to take the prisoners' place. They are 'justified' (Romans 5:1). The grace of God intervenes and we may know God's own lavish grace in our lives. The image in Romans 6:23 is graphic. The wages *(ipsona)* are what soldiers would receive as their earned pay, their just desserts. However the free gift *(dorean)* is the undeserved gift of eternal life for them. A *dorean* may be given at a special celebration, unearned and graciously given. The judgement we should receive, God in Christ gladly takes and sets us free. We are justified.

Relationships in the home

The image here is of the home with family and friends and, in particular, our relationship with the father (Romans 5:9-11). Its focus is reconciliation in which "in Christ God was reconciling the world to himself" (2 Corinthians 5:19). What is offered is a new relationship with God in which we may talk to God using the intimate term *Abba* (daddy). The response of faith to the grace of God means that we are 'adopted' into the family of Christ (John 1:12-13; Ephesians 1:5; 1 John 3:1-10). To be reconciled with Christ is to come within his challenging and transforming holy love (Ephesians 2:17-18).

A new relationship with God means a new relationship with the people of God (Ephesians 2:11-22). Racism and sexism are challenged, and status is irrelevant among the reconciled people of God. Indeed, there is a new relationship with all things (Colossians 1:15-20). God in Christ comes to reconcile the whole cosmos, which has been ruptured by sin.

Renewal of life

The word Paul uses to sum up the difference Jesus makes by his death and resurrection is 'metamorphosis', which we know in English and is translated in our Bibles as 'transformation'. Metamorphosis is what happens to a caterpillar when it comes a butterfly, and it is this kind of transforming difference the Resurrection makes. As Jesus was raised from the dead on that first Easter Day, and transformed, so our lives are transformed by his grace.

The Christian life is about renewal: that is, people becoming what God intended for them; the best they can be. It is not just about individuals but also about personal and social transformation.

7. Which image helps give you some understanding into the meaning of Jesus' death on the Cross?

8. Look back over the list of words and phrases you noted (see page 36). Share with others in the group the way these words are used today. What do they convey to you about the difference Jesus makes for people today?

A grandmother told this story:

Thirteen years ago my granddaughter, then five months old, was in hospital fighting for her life. She had the deadliest form of meningitis, and septicaemia had taken hold. The purple rash which had covered her skin had erupted into open wounds like craters all over her body. Sedated, lying naked in her cot, she was a pitiful sight. As I stood by her cot appalled by her terrible condition and racked with anguished love I sent up to God one of the most heartfelt prayers I have ever prayed. "God", I pleaded, "give these wounds to me. I would gladly take them in my body if she could be healed." At that moment the room was full of the presence of God. It dawned on me that this was exactly what Jesus had done. Looking with love and anguish on a desperately sick world he willingly offered himself and it was as if I heard him saying "Father, give these wounds to me. I would gladly take them in my body if they could be healed."

My granddaughter lived. Though still bearing the scars, she is a happy and healthy teenager.

My faith is that in the Cross we are seeing not the will of God but the nature of God – total self-giving love. Jesus and the Father are one.

Methodist emphasis

For all
What are known as the 'four alls of Methodism' (sometimes called 'Wesley's four alls') were not written by John Wesley, but used later to summarise his teaching and his view of what Jesus has done for us.

These are expressed as:
- all need to be saved
- all may be saved
- all may know themselves saved
- all may be saved to the uttermost.

 9. How do you respond to these themes?

10. How do you see evidence of them operating in the life of churches you know?

7

8

9

10

Holy Communion

This is a vitally important act within worship. During Holy Communion the minister retells what Jesus did for us on the Cross, that he rose again and lives for evermore. And as we are handed bread and wine we are reminded of his sacrifice for us, and for our need to respond to him.

As part of Holy Communion the people are invited to receive the bread and wine, with words such as these:

> *Come to this sacred table,*
> *not because you must but because you may;*
> *come, not to declare that you are righteous,*
> *but that you desire to be a true disciple of our Lord Jesus Christ:*
> *come, not because you are strong,*
> *but because you are weak;*
> *not because you have any claim on heaven's rewards,*
> *but because in your frailty and sin you stand in constant need of heaven's mercy and help.*

Methodist Worship Book, p. 158

11. If you have taken Holy Communion, what has it meant for you?

12. Having spent some time exploring what Jesus has done, how does Holy Communion take on a new or different meaning?

13. How would you encourage someone to receive Communion who says, "I am not worthy"?

Prayer reflection: confession and forgiveness

Act of confession

At the foot of the cross there is a bowl of warm water.

As you are given a sugar lump, be aware that it is made up of many small particles.

Sin affects and spoils our lives; it builds up and separates us from God and other people.

Spend a couple of minutes in quietness naming silently to God those things you want to confess (say sorry for).

Then drop the sugar lumps into a bowl of (warm) water perhaps with the words, "I am sorry God".

Receive God's forgiveness as you watch the sugar dissolve.

11

12

13

*For as the heavens are high above the
earth,
so great is his steadfast love towards
those who fear him;
as far as the east is from the west,
so far he removes our transgressions
from us.*

Psalm 103:11-12

Pray together:

**Magnificent God.
Thank you for all you have done for us in
Jesus,
for his risen life, alive in us today.
Help us by your Holy Spirit to walk in
newness of life,
humbly assured that we are made clean
by his death
and delighted to share his risen life with
others. Amen.**

Prayers of confession

(These are taken from the Holy
Communion service for Lent in the
Methodist Worship Book (pp. 148-149).)

Let us pray.
**Lord, you are steadfast in your love
and infinite in your mercy;
you welcome sinners
and invite them to be your guests.
We confess our sins,
trusting in you to forgive us.**

(Silence)

We have yielded to temptation and sinned:

Lord, have mercy.
Lord, have mercy.

*We have turned from our neighbours in
their need:*

Christ, have mercy.
Christ, have mercy.

We have resisted your word in our hearts:

Lord, have mercy.
Lord, have mercy.

*The almighty and most merciful God
grant you pardon,
forgiveness of all your sins,
time for true repentance
and amendment of life,
and the grace and comfort
of the Holy Spirit.* **Amen.**

After the assurance of forgiveness pray
together:

**Magnificent God.
Thank you for all you have done for us in
Jesus,
for his risen life, alive in us today.
Help us by your Holy Spirit to walk in
newness of life,**

*humbly assured that we are made clean
by his death
and delighted to share his risen life with
others. Amen.*

A Bible passage
to look at this week

*For as the heavens are high above the
earth,
so great is his steadfast love towards
those who fear him;
as far as the east is from the west,
so far he removes our transgressions
from us.*

Psalm 103:11-12

Prayer to use this week

Have a look around you this week (at
home, work, the neighbourhood and wider
world) and see where the transformation
that Jesus offers is needed. Maybe you
could offer a prayer for that situation:

*God of compassion and justice,
I bring before you ...
May your transforming love
bring healing and hope
within this situation
for Jesus' sake. Amen.*

To think about:
the four alls

All need to be saved

Everyone is in need of God's saving love
and no one can save themselves. In
Wesley's day, and ours, people generally
did not see that, so he emphasised it. As
Paul puts it writing to the Romans:

*There is no one who is righteous, not
even one;
there is no one who has understanding,
there is no one who seeks God.
All have turned aside ...*

Romans 3:10-12

This is linked to the notion that God is
there for us, before we ever realise it.

*Your sovereign grace to all extends
immense and unconfined;
from age to age it never ends;
enfolds all humankind.*

*Charles Wesley (1707-1788)
(Singing the Faith 436, v.2)*

All may be saved

Here is one of Methodism's distinctive
emphases. John Wesley followed the
teaching of a Dutch theologian, Jacobus
Arminius (so sometimes Methodists are
called Arminians), who taught that God's
grace was for all people. This is unlike
some Calvinists (following John Calvin

of Geneva) who believed that only the chosen (the elect) are to be saved and that others cannot be.

John Wesley was convinced that God invited everyone, though people may choose not to receive the invitation to salvation. Again Paul's words seem to convey that idea when he writes,

> For the love of Christ urges us on, because we are convinced that one has died for all; therefore all have died.

> 2 Corinthians 5:14

It is also implicit in many of the parables of Jesus about the banquet feast to which the poor and the outcast are invited to take their place (eg Matthew 22:2-14). Charles Wesley's hymn put it like this:

> O for a trumpet voice
> on all the world to call,
> to bid their hearts rejoice
> in him who died for all!
> For all my Lord was crucified,
> for all, for all my Saviour died.

> Charles Wesley (1707-1788)
> (Singing the Faith 358, v.7)

All may know themselves saved

This is the conviction that all Christians can know the love of God in their own hearts and minds. John Wesley referred to Paul's words in Romans 8 to support

his belief that God's Spirit witnesses with our spirit that we are children of God. This is sometimes called the 'doctrine of assurance'.

> For all who are led by the Spirit of God are children of God. For you did not receive a spirit of slavery to fall back into fear, but you have received a spirit of adoption. When we cry, "Abba! Father!" it is that very Spirit bearing witness with our spirit that we are children of God, and if children, then heirs, heirs of God and joint heirs with Christ – if, in fact, we suffer with him so that we may also be glorified with him.

> Romans 8:14-17

> My God, I am thine;
> what a comfort divine,
> what a blessing to know that my Jesus is mine!
> In the heavenly Lamb
> thrice happy I am,
> and my heart it doth dance at the sound of his name.

> Charles Wesley (1707-1788)
> (Singing the Faith 80, v.1)

All may be saved to the uttermost

This statement expresses well the notion that God is continually working in and through us by the Holy Spirit. We will look in more detail at this in Session 4, but at its heart it is about being filled with the transforming love of God. God is at work in and through us to draw us into God's own life and to make us complete or mature in Christ. This is sometimes called 'sanctification'.

> *Give me a new, a perfect heart,*
> *free from all doubt and fear at last;*
> *the mind which was in Christ impart,*
> *and let my spirit hold you fast.*
>
> *Now let me gain perfection's height,*
> *now let me into nothing fall,*
> *be less than nothing in thy sight,*
> *and feel that Christ is all in all.*

Charles Wesley (1707-1788)
(Singing the Faith 498, vv.4,6)

Session 4:
Empowered by the Holy Spirit

Opening prayer

Empowering God,
we are amazed at the love you show us
*   in Jesus,*
and would like to live out such love
*   ourselves.*
We know we need your power to live
*   differently,*
and be transformed people equipped
*   to serve you and others.*
Give us faith to receive your love,
and the power and presence of your
*   Holy Spirit in our lives.*
Bring through your irrepressible Spirit
*   a deeper understanding*
of all you can do in and through us.
Hear our prayer. Amen.

Welcome

In pairs, share briefly one insight you have gained so far in journeying with *Compass*.

Introduction

What kind of vehicles do people in the group have – or would like? Imagine such a car without an engine! In looking at the Holy Spirit we are looking at the 'engine' of the Church. In this session we explore what it means to seek 'the power of godliness'.

To make sense of the biblical passages about the Holy Spirit, let us first think about a big theme across the Bible. Big is the word for it, as it is about God: Father, Son and Holy Spirit.

Throughout the Scriptures from the beginning of Genesis, God is revealed to us as one God but as three in community. Andrei Rublev, the celebrated Russian painter, reflected this in his painting using the biblical story about the visit by three angels to the prophet Abraham and his wife Sarah (Genesis 18:1-8).

Sophie Hacker's interpretation of Rublev's icon is opposite. You can view an image of Rublev's original at www.googleartproject.com/collection/the-state-tretyakov-gallery/artwork/holy-trinity-troitsa-andrey-rublev/324417.

The angels are set as the three persons of the Trinity: God the Father, God the Son and God the Holy Spirit. In Rublev's original, the icon has the three angels shown equal. Art historians believe that it expresses the need for and benefit of love, of a union based on the trust of one individual in another. The image has a subtle balance between soul and spirit, the bodily form and the imponderable, endless and immortal themes. When speaking of Rublev's work, authors describe the Trinity's angels as quiet, gentle, anxious, sorrowful, and the mood permeating the icon as detached, meditative, contemplative and intimate.

Note how the angels are both similar and yet distinct, and how the light in the painting makes all three vital in the composition. Their attitudes, meaningful gestures and inclinations suggest an impression of a shared experience.

Note, too, how the angels interface with one another.

1. As you look at this icon, what do you see?

2. What do you think the icon is seeking to say about God: Father, Son and Holy Spirit?

Images of the Holy Spirit

The Bible suggests a number of images for the Holy Spirit:

- wind
- fire
- breath
- dove
- advocate
- counsellor
- helper
- strengthener

3. What do these images mean to you?

In the Old Testament the word for Spirit is *ruach* (Hebrew meaning wind, breath, spirit). In the New Testament it is translated *pneuma* (Greek) and carries the same meaning.

In addition, in John's Gospel we have the Greek word *parakletos*, which has a number of meanings:

- someone called to render some service, therefore the Holy Spirit is essentially a helper (counsellor)
- that which keeps a person on their feet when, left to themselves, they would collapse, a strengthener (comforter)
- the friend who bears witness in court to a friend's character when most needed, and when others wished to condemn; an advocate

1

2

3

wind ....

fire ....

breath...

dove ....

advocate...

counsellor...

helper...

strengthener..

- the word for calling people to noble deeds and high thoughts, who calls us to follow in God's mission in the world, the exhorter.

Take your modelling clay (or flour dough) and form a shape which reflects the image you have of the Holy Spirit. Spend a little time doing this and then talk about what your model represents. All modelling has different responses for people, so ask others in the group to respond to your model and share what they see in it.

Encountering the word

In this session we use a method of understanding the text which will help us to identify the key moments in the passage.

As the passage is read ask yourself: what are we discovering about the Holy Spirit as we reflect on these passages?

Mark any questions you have (with a question mark).

Circle what you consider to be the key words in the passage.

In pairs read some or all of the passages and, using the points above, consider the passages and report to the group.

Genesis 1:1-4 (Creation)

In the beginning when God created the heavens and the earth, the earth was a formless void and darkness covered the face of the deep, while a wind from God swept over the face of the waters. Then God said, "Let there be light"; and there was light. And God saw that the light was good; and God separated the light from the darkness.

Jeremiah 31:31-34 (A new covenant)

The days are surely coming, says the Lord, when I will make a new covenant with the house of Israel and the house of Judah. It will not be like the covenant that I made with their ancestors when I took them by the hand to bring them out of the land of Egypt – a covenant that they broke, though I was their husband, says the Lord. But this is the covenant that I will make with the house of Israel after those days, says the Lord: I will put my law within them, and I will write it on their hearts; and I will be their God, and they shall be my people. No longer shall they teach one another, or say to each other, "Know the Lord," for they shall all know me, from the least of them to the greatest, says the Lord; for I will forgive their iniquity, and remember their sin no more.

Joel 2:28-29
(God's Spirit poured out)

Then afterward
I will pour out my spirit on all flesh;
your sons and your daughters shall
prophesy,
your old men shall dream dreams,
and your young men shall see visions.
Even on the male and female slaves,
in those days, I will pour out my spirit.

Mark 1:9-13
(The Baptism of Jesus)

In those days Jesus came from
Nazareth of Galilee and was baptized by
John in the Jordan. And just as he was
coming up out of the water, he saw the
heavens torn apart and the Spirit
descending like a dove on him. And a voice
came from heaven, "You are my Son, the
Beloved; with you I am well pleased."

And the Spirit immediately drove him
out into the wilderness. He was in the
wilderness forty days, tempted by Satan;
and he was with the wild beasts; and the
angels waited on him.

Acts 2:1-8
(The coming of the Holy Spirit)

When the day of Pentecost had
come, they were all together in one place.
And suddenly from heaven there came a
sound like the rush of a violent wind, and
it filled the entire house where they were
sitting. Divided tongues, as of fire,
appeared among them, and a tongue
rested on each of them. All of them were
filled with the Holy Spirit and began to
speak in other languages, as the Spirit
gave them ability.

Now there were devout Jews from every
nation under heaven living in Jerusalem.
And at this sound the crowd gathered and
was bewildered, because each one heard
them speaking in the native language of
each. Amazed and astonished, they asked,
"Are not all these who are speaking
Galileans? And how is it that we hear, each
of us, in our own native language?"

[**Additional option: immersion in the text**
Read the whole passage (Acts 2:1-39) with
different people reading a paragraph.]

(The Jews kept the Feast of Pentecost,
50 days after the second day of Passover
(Leviticus 23:15-16). It was often called
the Feast of Weeks, and was traditionally
a joyous time of giving thanks to the Lord
and presenting offerings for the new grain
of the summer wheat harvest in Israel.)

The Methodist emphasis

Prevenient grace

In all Methodist theology there is the
biblical notion that God the Holy Spirit is
always moving ahead of us. God does not
force us; rather God allows free will but

anticipates our desire. Pre-venient means grace which is coming before, and coming ahead of us. Grace in this sense is the undeserved, transforming love of God which runs to meet us.

John Wesley emphasised that God offers a relationship. God has made the first move in Jesus and now it is time for us to respond. Divine grace led Jesus to the Cross because God wanted and wants to have a relationship with us.

Wesley was clear that God the Holy Spirit was at work in the lives of men and women for the illumination of the mind, the inclination of the will and desire for ultimate meaning. This is the Holy Spirit of God prompting, nudging and encouraging people in their reflection on the good news of Jesus and the possibility of a relationship with God.

 Reflect on your experience of God the Holy Spirit 'nudging' you to reflect on Christian faith.

4. What are the impulses that have prompted you to come to Compass?

5. In what ways has God has prepared you for this?

Prayers of confirmation

The Methodist Baptism services have a format different from other traditions, one which reflects this prevenient grace. The service first declares the grace of God, invites an affirmation of faith and then the person is received in Baptism and embraced in God's family. It is only after the Baptism that promises are made. Those involved in the Baptism, those supporting and the congregation all make their promises. The emphasis is that Baptism is dependent on God's grace.

Where people have been baptized as a child and seek Confirmation, or straight away when people are baptized as adults, there are prayers of confirmation. In the Confirmation service, as people are received into membership of the Methodist Church the minister prays:

By your power and grace, Lord,
strengthen these your servants,
that they may live as faithful disciples
    of Jesus Christ.
Increase in them your gifts of grace,
and fill them with your Holy Spirit:
the Spirit of wisdom and understanding;
the Spirit of discernment and inner
    strength;
the Spirit of knowledge, holiness,
    and awe.

Then the minister lays hands upon the head of each candidate, saying:

*Lord, confirm your servant (name)
by your Holy Spirit that she/he may
continue yours for ever. Amen.*

Methodist Worship Book, p. 100

 **In Baptism the emphasis is that
God has chosen you, whereas in
Confirmation you affirm that you
have chosen to follow Jesus. The prayers**

**are also that God should confirm God's
own blessing on you by the Holy Spirit.
What would this mean for you?**

The character of a Methodist

John Wesley was always being criticised
about 'the people called Methodist' and
so he wrote about the kind of people he
hoped Methodists would become:

4

5

You ask what I would do with them. I would make them virtuous and happy, easy in themselves and useful to others. Where would I lead them? To heaven – to God the judge, the lover of all, and to Jesus the mediator of the new Covenant. What religion do I preach? The religion of love – the law of kindness brought to light by the gospel. What is this good for? To make all who receive it enjoy God and themselves, to make them, like God, lovers of all, contented in their lives and crying out at their death, in calm assurance, "O grave where is thy victory? … Thanks be unto God, who giveth me victory, through my Lord Jesus Christ."

John Wesley, An earnest appeal to men of reason and religion, 1743

 6. How would you describe the character of a 'spirit-filled' Methodist?

Returning to Acts 2

In response to Peter's sermon (Acts 2:37) the people ask, 'What should we do?'

Peter replies in Acts 2:38-39:

Repent, and be baptized every one of you in the name of Jesus Christ so that your sins may be forgiven; and you will receive the gift of the Holy Spirit. For the promise is to you, for your children, and for all who are far away, everyone whom the Lord our God calls to him.

The people interrupt the sermon as they are exploring what it means to be a follower of Jesus. And there are some key thoughts in Peter's answer:

- **Repenting** – *metanioa* means to 'turn around', to start going in a different direction. So repentance is more than feeling or saying 'sorry'. It marks a new beginning with Christ and in our lives.

- **Receiving** – the Holy Spirit is God's supportive, encouraging and enabling gift to all who have faith in Jesus. The Holy Spirit will empower our lives.

- **Belonging** – the response of faith here is to be baptized, which is a sign of belonging to Christ and to the whole community of Christian faith.

 7. If the Christian pathway is a journey which involves all of these, how does your journey match these markers on the way?

At the beginning of this session we noted that looking at the Holy Spirit this week we are looking at the 'engine' of the Church.

At this point we need to recognise two truths which belong together. All who follow Jesus have received the Holy Spirit, but not all are filled with the Spirit.

6

7

All who follow Jesus have received the Spirit ...

> No one can say "Jesus is Lord" except by the Holy Spirit.
>
> *1 Corinthians 12:3*

> But you are not in the flesh; you are in the Spirit, since the Spirit of God dwells in you. Anyone who does not have the Spirit of Christ does not belong to him.
>
> *Romans 8:9*

... but not all are filled with the Spirit.

> Be filled with the Spirit, as you sing psalms and hymns and spiritual songs among yourselves, singing and making melody to the Lord in your hearts, giving thanks to God the Father at all times and for everything in the name of our Lord Jesus Christ.
>
> *Ephesians 5:18-20*

The appeal to "be filled with the Spirit" should be translated as 'be being filled with the Spirit' – it is a continuous process, like being continually filled with God's grace.

Prayer reflection: the work of the Spirit

Using a printed outline of a dove or a ribbon, write the names or situations you wish to pray for on the dove or ribbon. When you have finished, tie it onto a string or wire which has a fan behind.

Use this prayer from the Roman Catholic tradition, inviting the Holy Spirit to come to us. (This is called a prayer of invocation.)

> Come, Holy Spirit,
> fill the hearts of your faithful people,
> and kindle in them the fire of your love;
>
> Send forth your love and they shall be created,
> **and you shall renew the face of the earth.**
>
> O God,
> who by the light of the Holy Spirit
> did instruct the hearts of the faithful,
> grant that by the same Holy Spirit
> we may be truly wise and ever enjoy
> your consolations.
> Through Christ our Lord. **Amen.**

Someone then offers a prayer as the prayers are blown by the fan, illustrating the wind of the Spirit at work.

Prayers for each other

Take some time to pray for each other

that you may know the filling of the Holy Spirit in your lives. You could use this prayer now and during the week, that by God's Sprit, you will be filled with love, equipped for service and enabled in discipleship.

> Come Holy Spirit,
> fill my life with your love,
> guide my path with your truth,
> enable me to follow in Jesus' footsteps,
> this and every day. Amen.

 And finally ... if we are to be a community of people receiving the grace of the Father, following the way of Jesus and filled with the Holy Spirit, what are the implications for you and the church of which you are part?

A Bible passage to look at this week

> For all who are led by the Spirit of God are children of God. For you did not receive a spirit of slavery to fall back into fear, but you have received a spirit of adoption. When we cry, "Abba! Father!" it is that very Spirit bearing witness with our spirit that we are children of God, and if children, then heirs, heirs of God and joint heirs with Christ – if, in fact, we suffer with him so that we may also be glorified with him.
>
> Romans 8:14-17

To think about: assurance and holiness

At the heart of John Wesley's teaching was a response to God's grace. Wesley was concerned that the people called Methodist should know the assurance of sins forgiven. His own experience led him to this. He had been devoted to God and his calling but it was the experience of grace he noted in his journal of 24 May 1738:

> In the evening I went very unwillingly to a society in Aldersgate Street, where one was reading Luther's preface to the Epistle to the Romans. About a quarter before nine, while he was describing the change which God works in the heart through faith in Christ, I felt my heart strangely warmed. I felt I did trust in Christ, Christ alone, for salvation; and an assurance was given me that he had taken away my sins, even mine, and saved me from the law of sin and death.

Wesley wanted people to know that while we stand in awe of God, we can also know that we are 'children of God', adopted into God's family. There is both awe and intimacy in this relationship. Paul writes:

> When we cry "Abba! Father!" it is that very Spirit bearing witness with our spirit that we are children of God.
>
> Romans 8:16

Ask any Christian and they will say that their sense of assurance goes up and down, like any relationship, but one of the Methodist emphases is that we may know we are saved.

Wesley's answers to the questions about holiness, or perfection as it was sometimes called, are revealing:

- "What is implied in being a perfect Christian?" was one of the questions asked when the doctrine was discussed at the first Methodist Conference in 1744. This was the answer given: "The loving the Lord our God with all our heart, and with all our mind, and soul, and strength" (Deuteronomy 6:5; 30:6; Ezekiel 36:25-29).
- "All that is necessarily implied therein [ie in Christian Perfection]," Wesley explained to Hannah Ball, the pioneer of Methodist Sunday Schools, "is humble, gentle, patient love, love regulating all the tempers and governing all the words and actions."
- In John Wesley's sermon *The Scripture way of salvation* (1765), he writes, "But what is perfection? The word has various senses: here it means perfect love. It is love excluding sin; love filling the heart, taking up the whole capacity of the same."

- That statement is confirmed in his letter to Walter Churchey in 1771: "Entire sanctification, or Christian perfection, is neither more nor less than pure love – love expelling sin and governing both the heart and life of a child of God".

These were the terms Wesley employed to express the heart of what he meant about holiness. Holiness was being so filled with the love of God that there was no room for anything else, prompted and guided by love.

So Christian holiness is:
- not absolute (God's perfection is unequalled)
- not sinless (only Jesus was without sin)
- not infallible (not free from ignorance or mistakes)
- not free from temptation (even Jesus was tempted)
- not free from infirmities (such as dullness of thought or slowness of speed)
- not final (there is always room for growth).

Holiness for Wesley was also not just about a spiritual experience, but how that was worked out in everyday life. After all, if holiness is about being filled with the love of God, then it should have implications. All his guidance to preachers, sharing in small groups, starting schools, opening orphanages, publishing advice on medicine in a booklet called *Primitive Physic* so people were not exploited by the medics of the day, flowed from his committed belief that being filled with the love of God had implications for the way we live and how we deal with others.

This emphasis on holiness as the relationship with God is also the basis for Wesley's view of assurance. "All may know themselves saved" was a significant part of Wesley's view of salvation (see Session 3, page 44). That we could know the love of God as a deep and intense experience is the grounds of such knowing, and of being sure.

To think about: what does the Bible say about the Holy Spirit?

The Spirit enabling the Church

We have already seen that the Holy Spirit was involved throughout Scripture. But at Pentecost the Spirit came in a new and fuller way. The presence of the Holy Spirit is the hallmark of the Christian (Acts 19:2) and of the Christian community (Acts 8). The Spirit's presence and faith in Jesus are connected, for "no one can say 'Jesus is Lord' except by the Holy Spirit" (1 Corinthians 12:3).

We often think of the work of the Spirit as being solely in the life of the believer, but the Bible teaches us that the Spirit is active before we come to believe. For example, the very preaching of the gospel (good news of Jesus) is done by or in the Holy Spirit (1 Peter 1:12) and its content is revealed by the Spirit (Ephesians 3:5); when people are convicted of sin, that is a work of the Spirit (John 16:8-9); the Christian life is begun in the Spirit (Galatians 3:3). People are saved, "not because of any works of righteousness that we had done, but according to his mercy, through the water of rebirth and renewal by the Holy Spirit" (Titus 3:5). God is at work before ever we know it.

Fruit of the Spirit

Reference to fruit and fruit-bearing is found throughout the New Testament and, when used in the sense of spiritual fruit, is the result of the power of the Spirit working in those who turn to God. The true disciple will be known by their 'fruits' (John 15:8); the character of a person reveals their inmost motivation.

If our motivation in life is to love Christ and to serve him in the power of the Spirit, then our character will be infused with his love. So it is clear that when we live in the orbit of the Spirit's work, alive to and walking with the Spirit, this fruit will be seen in our lives. Such fruit comes from obedient living which resonates with the life of Jesus and his demands upon us.

The fruit of the Spirit (Galatians 5:22-23) can be seen in:

- **Love**, **joy** and **peace** which describe the Christian's experience in relation to God and in what we receive from God. Love is in all other fruit; joy springs from assurance of our relationship with God in Christ and is an overflow of Christian gladness, even in the face of distress or difficulty; peace is deep-seated, arising from confidence in God, and carries the notion of harmony and 'stands guard' over heart and mind.
- **Patience**, **kindness** and **goodness** which describe the Christian's experience in relation to others – our attitude. Patience means being prepared to wait with a good temper and includes ideas of long-suffering and endurance; kindness is being good-hearted or well disposed towards others, not stern; goodness expresses itself in deeds which benefit others.
- **Faithfulness**, **gentleness** and **self-control** which describe the Christian's experience in relation to one's self – our inner response. Faithfulness refers to reliability and trustworthiness; gentleness includes ideas of lowliness and humility, but this gentleness is strong, not weak. Self-control refers to personal discipline of self and passions.

Gifts of the Spirit

The word used in the New Testament is *charismata* – gift of grace, or love gift – and is used to identify those gifts and skills which are beneficial for Christian communities.

There are three places where various gifts are listed: Romans 12; 1 Corinthians 12; Ephesians 4.

The gifts of the Spirit are not given merely for personal enrichment but "for the common good" (1 Corinthians 12:7). In asking his readers to use their *charisma* for the good of others, Peter assumes that each Christian has a gift to employ in the service of God (1 Peter 4:10). Some distinguish between what they call ordinary gifts, such as administration, and dramatic gifts such as tongues, healing or prophecy. However this is not a distinction made by the New Testament which clearly thought of all love gifts as being given by "the same Spirit" (1 Corinthians 12:11). All the gifts given by Christ are necessary for the complete functioning of his body, the Church. Where we refuse to recognise and use these gifts, the ministry of the Church will be impoverished.

Session 5: Life together

Opening prayer

Caring God,
we have glimpsed you in our own stories,
heard of your love for us in Jesus
and been humbled by the story of his
death.
Encouraged by the power of your Spirit,
today we offer you our life together.
May the quality of our worship,
relationships with each other, and caring
for others,
hold us in your truth
and enable others to glimpse good news.
Hear our prayer. Amen.

Welcome

Looking back over recent weeks, what do you think God is doing in your life?

Introduction

Think of the Church like a vehicle or vessel – what kind of vehicle or vessel would it be? A car, an ambulance, a sailing ship?

> *"For me it would be a Citroen 2CV – I am the proud owner of a green and white Dolly. It is a bit battered but I lavish loving care on it and it runs well, serving all kinds of purposes and people. When people see it some smile with recognition, others look with pity."*
>
> Howard Mellor

Here are two quite different images, one drawn as part of the handwritten Bible project in 2011 and one written years ago:

from the Methodist Church's Handwritten Bible Project in 2011, Matthew chapter 15, Mumbles Methodist Church, Swansea © TMCP.

"Such a [Methodist] Society is no other than 'a company of [people], having the form, and seeking the power, of godliness; united, in order to pray together, to receive the word of exhortation, and to watch over one another in love, that they may help each other to work out their salvation.'"

from the Wesley's 'Rules of the Society', 1743, CPD Volume 1 (Peterborough, Methodist Publishing, 1988), p.73

People have used many different images to describe the Church:

- advice centre
- petrol station
- rock
- fortress
- circus
- social club
- lifeboat station
- museum
- maze
- team
- Spaghetti Junction
- orchestra
- lighthouse
- A&E department
- field
- bus-stop queue
- tree
- pyramid
- weaving
- bread

How do you relate to them? Which ones attract you most? Why?
Which ones do you find difficult to relate to as 'church'? Why?

Encountering the word

Acts 2:42-47
They devoted themselves to the apostles' teaching and fellowship, to the breaking of bread and the prayers. Awe came upon everyone, because many wonders and signs were being done by the apostles. All who believed were together and had all things in common; they would sell their possessions and goods and distribute the proceeds to all, as any had need. Day by day, as they spent much time together in the temple, they broke bread at home and ate their food with glad and generous hearts, praising God and having the goodwill of all the people. And day by day the Lord added to their number those who were being saved.

In groups of two or three look at the Acts passage. Whatever we feel about this description, it certainly is not boring!

1a. What are 'the church' or 'the believers' doing or being asked to do in the passage?

1b. Who will benefit from the activity which is described?

1c. Which of the images you discussed earlier do you find in this passage?

1

a ....

....

....

....

....

....

b ....

....

....

....

....

....

c ....

....

....

....

....

....

Acts 2 describes a Christian community of people who share many things.

Think of the church you know best.

2a. How connected do you feel to others?

2b. What can you contribute to the life of your Christian community?

2c. How can we celebrate the different gifts God has given?

"Church is not something you show up to and consume, you have to be a contributor, a participant." How do you react to this statement?

Images of Church in the Bible

Astonishingly there are 96 different images or analogies of the Church in the New Testament. Prepare to read these texts and listen carefully. Then at the end of each section hold your thoughts in silence.

Some images are organic:
- the Body of Christ (Romans 12:4-5; 1 Corinthians 12:27; Ephesians 4:11-16)
- fishers for people (Mark 1:17)
- branches of the vine (John 15:5)
- the bride of Christ (Ephesians 5:23-32)
- a flock (Luke 12:32; John 10:16).

The Church is more of an organism than an organisation; a living body indwelt by the Holy Spirit. These images suggest mutual interdependence of the community, the variety of gifts for the enrichment and benefit of the whole community.

Some images are structural:
- the field/building of God (1 Corinthians 3:9)
- a building on a rock (Matthew 16:18)
- the salt of the earth (Matthew 5:13)
- a letter of Christ (2 Corinthians 3:2-3)
- a new Jerusalem (Revelation 21:2)
- a building (Ephesians 2:19-22; 1 Peter 2:5).

These images suggest a community that offers sanctuary, is integrated and transforms the community around it.

Some images are relational:
- the household of God (Ephesians 2:19)
- citizens of heaven (Philippians 3:20)
- a society of friends (John 15:12-17)
- the poor (Luke 6:20)
- God's own people (1 Peter 2:9) (or as in the King James Version, 'God's peculiar people'!).

A function of this group of images is to see the Christian community as a pilgrim people drawing on the covenant promises of the Old Testament.

3. Which of these images, from your point of view, seem appropriate today? Why?

 Share some of your thoughts with your neighbour.

2

a ....
....
....

b ....
....
....

c ....
....
....

3

....
....
....
....
....
....

Called out!

In the New Testament Greek the word used to describe the community of believers is *Ekklesia* (meaning 'to call out'). So the Church is an assembly or a 'called out' company.

The word is used to describe a particular congregation (1 Corinthians 14:19,34), a body of Christians in one city (Acts 11:22; 13:1) or all Christians everywhere (Ephesians 5:23). *Ekklesia* is also on the lips of Jesus (Matthew 16:18; 18:17).

The Church is also a fellowship of those who are 'in Christ', and being 'in Christ' are in fellowship with all others who are 'in Christ'. Each local fellowship of believers is a microcosm of the global Church.

Empowered and guided by the Spirit, the Christian community is God's new creation, the first signs of God's new humanity which points towards a radical new beginning (Acts 2:17-21; Galatians 3:28).

In all of this the Church is a servant people (Matthew 20:25-26; Mark 10:45; 2 Corinthians 4:5), and the Christian community is outward-looking to serve God and the world created by God.

 4a. How is your church (and how are you!) called to speak out the good news of Jesus in your community?

4b. What kind of contributions could you make to the church you know best?

4c. What do you think the Church is for?

4

a ....

....

b ....

....

c ....

....

What is your experience of Church so far?

The list below includes a variety of the texts in the New Testament which include the phrase "one another". What kind of Church would it be if these were all true in your church?

How do you think the church you know best scores? Circle the smiley face for 'well', sad face for 'poorly' or straight-faced for 'not sure'.

Let us therefore no longer pass judgement on one another, but resolve instead never to put a stumbling block in the way of another. *Romans 14:13*	☺ ☺ ☹
Welcome one another, therefore, just as Christ has welcomed you, for the Glory of God. *Romans 15:7*	☺ ☺ ☹
Have the same care for one another. *1 Corinthians 12:25*	☺ ☺ ☹
Bear one another's burdens, and in this way you will fulfil the law of Christ. *Galatians 6:2*	☺ ☺ ☹
Be kind to one another. *Ephesians 4:32*	☺ ☺ ☹
Do not lie to one another. *Colossians 3:9*	☺ ☺ ☹
Bear with one another and, if anyone has a complaint against another, forgive each other; just as the Lord has forgiven you so you also must forgive. *Colossians 3:13*	☺ ☺ ☹
Teach and admonish one another in all wisdom. *Colossians 3:16*	☺ ☺ ☹
Let us consider how to provoke one another to love and good deeds. *Hebrews 10:24*	☺ ☺ ☹
Confess your sins to one another, and pray for one another. *James 5:16*	☺ ☺ ☹
Clothe yourselves with humility in your dealings with one another. *1 Peter 5:5*	☺ ☺ ☹
For this is the message you have heard from the beginning, that we should love one another. *1 John 3:11*	☺ ☺ ☹

The Methodist emphasis

A Methodist story

The early Methodist history is a dramatic story of growth presided over by John Wesley, but after his death the movement splintered into many streams (Wesleyan Methodist, Primitive Methodist, United Methodist, Methodist New Connexion and Bible Christian, etc). Most came together to form the Methodist Church in Britain in 1932. Strands of the Methodist movement which started in the nineteenth century and are still internationally renowned today are the Salvation Army and the Church of the Nazarene. The Wesleyan Reform Union also remains in parts of Britain. But what is most important to remember is that the Methodist Church is made up of people of faith.

The Confirmation promises

In the last session (page 52) we considered part of the Confirmation service.

After the confirming prayer praying that God by the Holy Spirit will bless them, there are promises for those being confirmed and promises by the whole congregation:

The minister says to *those* newly-confirmed:

N and N (N),
I ask you now to respond to God's love and grace by making these promises.

Will you commit yourself to the Christian life of worship and service, and be open to the renewing power of God?
With God's help I will.

Will you seek the strength of God's Spirit as you accept the cost of following Jesus Christ in your daily life?
With God's help I will.

Will you witness, by word and deed, to the good news of God in Christ, and so bring glory to God?
With God's help I will.

The minister says to the people:

Members of the body of Christ, we rejoice that these, our sisters and brothers, have been confirmed.

Will you so maintain the Church's life of worship and service that they may grow in grace and in the knowledge and love of God and of his Son Jesus Christ our Lord?
With God's help we will.

[Then comes a prayer said by the whole congregation:]

Generous God,
touch us again
with the fire of your Spirit
and renew us by your grace,
that we may profess the one true faith
and live in love and unity
with all who follow Christ. Amen.

Methodist Worship Book, pp. 100-101

 5a. What do you think these promises commit someone to?

5b. What do you think is the relationship between belief and belonging?

Holy Communion

If we are committed to belonging to Christ, as the Confirmation promises indicate, we are also committing ourselves to sharing with other followers. One of the key moments which celebrates our belonging to Christ and one another is in Holy Communion. John Wesley called upon Methodists to use what he called the "means of grace". And most important to him was receiving bread and wine at Holy Communion.

Here is part of the prayer of thanksgiving for Pentecost:

And so,
in remembrance of all his mighty acts,
we offer you these gifts,
and with them ourselves
as a holy, living sacrifice.

You send forth your Spirit.
You bind us in love.
You renew the face of the earth.

Pour out your Holy Spirit
that these gifts of bread and wine
may be for us the body and blood of Christ.
Unite us with him and with one another
in mission to all the world;
and bring us with the whole creation
to your heavenly kingdom.

5

a ....

....

b ....

....

Through Christ, with Christ, in Christ,
in the unity of the Holy Spirit,
all blessing and honour and glory
*   and power*
be yours for ever and ever. Amen.

Methodist Worship Book, p. 181

 6. Bread and wine are ordinary things to speak of the salvation Jesus offers. Why do you think he chose these simple elements?

 Holy Communion has different titles in Methodism: the Lord's Supper, Holy Communion, Breaking of Bread and Eucharist (meaning Thanksgiving). Why do you think all these titles may be used?

Part of the wider Church

We each have to work out what it means to be part of the worshipping Church and engaged in the community.

Did you know:

- one third of the world's population adheres to the Christian faith
- there are 80 million Methodists in the world
- it is now reckoned that there are more Christians in China than in all of Europe
- there are about 2,200 people engaged in ordained ministry in British Methodism today
- there are, in 2013, almost 5,000 local Methodist churches in Britain in just under 500 circuits
- 162 of the churches in British Methodism use a language other than English in their worship
- Methodism engages in education, with many day and boarding schools
- Methodists founded what today we know as Action for Children (formerly NCH - National Children's Home) and MHA (Methodist Homes for the Aged)?

figures correct in 2013

6

Prayer reflection: prayer plaits

Cut three equal lengths of wool or thin ribbon (about 9 inches or 22 cm long) in the colours of your choice. One colour represents yourself, another represents God, and the third represents other people.

Knot them together at one end.
Plait the wool as you reflect on your relationship with God and with others.

Knot the end when you finish and, as you do so, silently offer a prayer asking that you and all those you have thought of are held in God's love.

As a parting blessing, say together this prayer from the Iona Community which concludes a Holy Communion service:

Lord Jesus Christ,
You have put your life in our hands.
Now we put our lives in yours.
Take us, shake us, remake us;
no longer is what we have been important,
it is what we can be, with you, starting now. Amen.

Adapted from a prayer on page 101 of A Wee Worship Book (fourth incarnation) (Wild Goose Publications, 2004) © Wild Goose Resource Group, Iona Community, Glasgow G2 3DH. www.wgrg.co.uk. Used by permission.

A Bible passage to look at this week

May the God of steadfastness and encouragement grant you to live in harmony with one another, in accordance with Christ Jesus, so that together you may with one voice glorify the God and Father of our Lord Jesus Christ.

Romans 15:5-6

Prayer to use this week

Christ has no body now on earth but yours,
no hands, no feet but yours.
Yours are the eyes through which Christ looks compassion into the world,
yours are the feet, with which he is to go about doing good,
and yours are the hands with which Christ blesses the world.

Teresa of Avila (1515-1582)

The next meeting will focus on the Bible. If you have a Bible at home (particularly one that means a lot to you) then please bring it. There will be an opportunity during the session to 'introduce your Bible' and share why it means so much to you.

To think about: the Church

The Connexion

Methodists belong to local churches or ecumenical partnerships, but also feel part of a larger connected community, the Connexion. (You can find more information about the structure of the Methodist Church (including a diagram) at www.methodist.org.uk/who-we-are/structure.)

This sense of being connected makes a difference to how the Methodist Church as a whole is structured. At its heart is an understanding of the Christian community as the "Body of Christ". Just as a human body contains different limbs and organs that depend on each other, so we should be close and caring enough to feel each other's pain and delight. We should put the good of the whole body before our own individual needs.

"Do not allow yourself one thought of separating from your brothers and sisters, whether their opinions agree with yours or not."

John Wesley

The promise of mutual support is a strength of Methodism. If you become a member of the Methodist Church, a pastoral visitor is responsible for visiting you and offering spiritual support, encouragement and challenge.

In the Methodist Church decisions are made as openly as possible, giving opportunities for all to contribute. It is important for all views to be heard and taken seriously, especially where Christians disagree.

Four marks of the Church

The Church, as any traveller will tell you, is in every part of the world, with churches in the most unexpected places. Early on in the Church's history, people faced the question, "How do you describe the church?" There developed four classical marks of Church, though for each of them there is a flipside as well.

- **One**
  A unity (Ephesians 4:4-6); Jesus prayed that his disciples should be one (John 17:21, 23). The Church is often seen as a fellowship of churches, which confess our Lord Jesus Christ as God and Saviour. But the Church is also diverse, with some churches putting a strong emphasis on the importance of Holy Communion and some putting a strong emphasis on the importance of paying attention to the Holy Spirit in our worship and living. So it is unity in diversity.

- **Holy**
  There is a sanctity about it in that it is 'set apart' for God (1 Peter 2:9). The

Church is the dwelling place of the Holy Spirit (Ephesians 2:22). As God's instrument in the world, the members share the holiness of Jesus, the head (1 Corinthians 12:27; Colossians 1:18). But the Church is made up of sinners and saints, and it is set apart and also engaged in the community. To follow the way of Jesus it must be a 'friend of sinners'. In other words, it is holiness, but engaged in community.

- **Catholic (universal)**
  (This comes from the Greek *katholou*, referring to the whole. The Greek words were translated into the Latin *catholicus*.) Where Jesus Christ is, there is a catholic Church not limited by barriers of age, race, culture or gender (Matthew 28:19; Acts 10:34-35; Galatians 3:28; Revelation 5:9-10). But it also is local in its expression of worship and mission. So it is both global and local.

- **Apostolic**
  The Church is built on the foundation of apostles and prophets (Ephesians 2:20). Jesus entrusted his teaching to the twelve and all who follow. 'Apostolic' relates to the foundations of the faith laid down in the early Church. 'Apostolic' means we have roots. But the Church also focuses on mission as people 'being sent' to live

and speak of the truth of Christ. So it is both grounded in tradition and on the move with the gospel (good news of Jesus).

A new look at the Christian story:
This is the kind of conversation between two people who have never met before and, over coffee, are waiting in an airport lounge.

1 *Excuse me asking, but what is your job?*
2 *I work in the charity sector.*
1 *Oh really, what aspect of charity work?*
2 *My organisation is involved in personal and social transformation.*
1 *Gosh, that sounds fascinating. Is it international?*
2 *Yes, we are present in almost every country in the world.*
1 *My word – what kind of things do you do?*
2 *We are involved in community development, health care, especially for elderly and young people, family support, youth work, adult education and development. We sponsor universities, and campaign on justice issues. We have been at the forefront of the Fair Trade movement.*
1 *Golly, that is amazing. What do you do in this country?*
2 *We have small groups meeting daily and larger groups weekly. In 2013*

we have in Britain over 5,000 outlets and employ about 2,200 people to supervise and train volunteers.

1 **Wow, how many volunteers have you?**

2 Well, worldwide there are over 80 million and in the UK about 500,000.

1 **Good gracious! Tell me what is this organisation you work for?**

2 It's called the Methodist Church!

This form of telling the story of the Church's work is used by a number of people, but it owes its origin to an article in the *Ecumenical Review*. We often tell our story in a downbeat way – there used to be more of us, etc. However the story of the Church in our day is one of growth and development across the world.

Session 6: Engaging with Scripture

Opening prayer

Living God,
we find ourselves drawn into your
awesome mystery,
amazed and challenged by Jesus
and sensing the power of your Holy Spirit.
It can feel a little like standing on the edge
of a precipice,
drawn to throw in our lot with you,
yet holding back, unsure what it might
entail.
Today, we pray that the words of Scripture,
treasured by faithful generations before us,
may become life-giving words for us.
Hear our prayer. Amen.

Sculpture by Jude Price.
Creative Conundrums. Used with permission.
www.creativeconundrums.com/about/about-jude-price

Welcome

Reflecting on the last session, how can
you contribute to your local church?

Introduction

1. Look at the picture above of
a sculpture by Judith Price.
What does the image say about
the person and the book?

1

....

....

....

If you have brought a Bible with you, now is the time to introduce it.

- *Do you have a Bible – what kind?*
- *If you have more than one Bible, which one means the most to you?*
- *How did you receive this Bible?*
- *What particularly interesting Bibles have you seen?*
- *Describe a story told from the Bible that interested or surprised you.*

What do we know about the book?

1. How many books are in the Bible?
   a) 27
   b) 66
   c) 39

2. What does 'testament' mean?
   a) long exam
   b) parchment
   c) covenant

3. Who wrote the Bible?
   a) many different authors, inspired by the Holy Spirit, from all walks of life: shepherds, farmers, tent-makers, physicians, fishermen, priests, prophets, philosophers and kings
   b) the priestly, educated tribe of Israel and later priests in the early Church
   c) Moses and Dan Brown

4. About how long did it take to write the Bible?
   a) over 4,000 years, between 3500BC and AD500
   b) over 1,200 years, between 1100BC and AD100
   c) over 600 years, between 500BC to AD100

5. In what languages was the Bible written in?
   a) Cantonese and Swahili
   b) Hebrew, Aramaic, and Greek
   c) Latin and Coptic

6. When was the collection of books that makes up the Bible (the canon of Scripture) agreed? (Canon is derived from the Greek word *kaōn*, signifying a measuring rod or rule. It became the collection of writings accepted by the early Christian Church for use in Church as the basis for Christian reflection, remembrance and belief.)
   a) AD33
   b) AD367
   c) AD1966

7. When was the first translation of the Bible made into English?
   a) 1611, under the orders of King James I
   b) 1525 by William Tyndale
   c) 1382 by John Wycliffe

8. Underline which types of literature are found in the Bible.
   a) laws
   b) instruction on ritual
   c) history
   d) political argument
   e) wise sayings
   f) hymns
   g) poems
   h) laments
   i) curses
   j) Gospels (good news)
   k) stories
   l) parables
   m) myths
   n) prophetic writing
   o) correspondence
   p) apocalyptic writing

9. Roughly how many languages has the whole Bible been translated into?
   a) 5 languages
   b) 50 languages, the same as Shakespeare's works
   c) over 2,000 languages

10. Is the Bible the world's best-selling book?
    a) yes
    b) no
    c) no, but still selling very well

11. Where are most Bibles printed today?
    a) USA
    b) China
    c) UK

Encountering the word

The following quote is a useful lens to have as we approach the Scriptures. Bear it in mind as we go through the session.

> Christians do not believe **in** the Bible; they believe in the living God attested **by** the Bible. Scripture is indispensable in bringing us into a new relationship with the living God through Christ by the power of the Holy Spirit, and thus into new relationship with others and with the entire creation. To speak of the authority of the Bible rightly is to speak of its power by God's Spirit to help create and nourish this new life in relationship with God and with others.

Daniel L Migliore, Faith seeking understanding (William B Eerdmans Publishing Co, second revised edition 2004) Used by permission

Reading the Bible for the story
The overarching story of God creating the world and loving it is at the heart of Christian faith. The themed struggles of humans seeking and being found by God over thousands of years give a vocabulary to express our own searching.

 2. Take the names of people and the major events of the Bible and try to get them in the right order. While doing this, talk about the story of God's salvation to God's own people and supremely in Jesus. (It is not

crucial to get the exact order, but what questions emerge for you?)

So why do we have the Bible?

Here are some thoughts from the Bible.

Now Jesus did many other signs in the presence of his disciples, which are not written in this book. But these are written so that you may come to believe that Jesus is the Messiah, the Son of God, and that through believing you may have life in his name.

John 20:30-31

Your word is a lamp to my feet and a light to my path.

Psalm 119:105

Divine revelation

God's self-revelation comes through:

- the words and actions of Jesus
- the Bible
- the Christian community.

As followers of Jesus we are people who focus on Scripture who seek to interpret it for today. John Wesley said that he was a "man of one book", the Bible. But he also wrote lots and read widely as he sought to interpret the Bible. Divine revelation, the way God reveals God's own self, includes the Creeds and the heritage of the Church discerned over the ages.

A story we can be part of

This divine revelation is something in which we participate. There is a sense in which the Bible is an unfinished story. Not only does it point to God's fulfilment of history, but it is also a story we can be part of now.

John Wesley had a view about this. Commenting on 2 Timothy 3:16, he writes:

The Spirit of God not only once inspired those who wrote it [the Scriptures] but continually inspires, supernaturally assists, those who read it with earnest prayer.

Explanatory Notes Upon the New Testament
(London, Epworth, 1941), p. 794

This has been called Wesley's theory of double inspiration – inspired then and now.

But as for you, continue in what you have learned and firmly believed, knowing from whom you learned it, and how from childhood you have known the sacred writings that are able to instruct you for salvation through faith in Christ Jesus. All scripture is inspired by God and is useful for teaching, for reproof, for correction, and for training in righteousness, so that everyone who belongs to God may be proficient, equipped for every good work.

2 Timothy 3:14-17

3a. What things does this passage suggest are the purposes of Scripture?

3b. How do they relate to you?

3c. How then can we engage with Scripture?

In many ways the Bible is a toolbox for spiritual living; to transform our attitudes and lifestyle. We can read Scripture as a tool for prayer, as we pray for comfort, guidance, challenge and strength.

Three different ways of reading Scripture
Each way can lead you to a deep place in your reflection.

Reading Scripture and using the senses
We have a tendency to use just our minds to think about Scripture. But we can also engage our emotions by using

2

3

a ....

b ....

c ....

our imagination and all of our senses. What sounds, smells, tastes, sights and touches do the words evoke in you? What memories are brought back for you? How are God's words affecting you through your senses?

Mark 10:46-52

As you read the passage, imagine you are in the crowd. Think about what you might hear, see, smell, touch and taste.

They came to Jericho. As he and his disciples and a large crowd were leaving Jericho, Bartimaeus son of Timaeus, a blind beggar, was sitting by the roadside. When he heard that it was Jesus of Nazareth, he began to shout out and say, "Jesus, Son of David, have mercy on me!" Many sternly ordered him to be quiet, but he cried out even more loudly, "Son of David, have mercy on me!" Jesus stood still and said, "Call him here." And they called the blind man, saying to him, "Take heart; get up, he is calling you." So throwing off his cloak, he sprang up and came to Jesus. Then Jesus said to him, "What do you want me to do for you?" The blind man said to him, "My teacher, let me see again." Jesus said to him, "Go; your faith has made you well." Immediately he regained his sight and followed him on the way.

4a. What you are wearing? How hot is it? What you can hear, see or smell?

4b. Where are you in the crowd – on the edge, in the middle? Can you see Jesus? Can you see Bartimaeus?

4c. How do you feel when Bartimaeus shouts out?

4d. How do you feel when Bartimaeus is healed?

As you read the passage again, imagine you are Bartimaeus.

5a. What can you hear?

5b. How do you feel as Jesus approaches?

5c. How do you feel when Jesus stops and speaks to you?

6. Imagine Jesus standing before you now and asking the question, "What do you want me to do for you?" How do you (not Bartimaeus) answer?

Praying with Scripture

A crucial question in exploring faith is what it means to trust God. When life is hard, will we find the resources to cope?

4

a ....

....

b ....

....

c ....

....

d ....

....

5

a ....

....

b ....

....

c ....

....

6

....

....

Psalms are both a hymn and a prayer. For example, the writer of Psalm 23 believes that the resources are to hand, and God will sustain him.

Psalm 23

The Lord is my shepherd,
I shall not want.
He makes me lie down in green pastures;
he leads me beside still waters;
he restores my soul.
He leads me in right paths
for his name's sake.

Even though I walk through the darkest valley,
I fear no evil;
for you are with me;
your rod and your staff—
they comfort me.
You prepare a table before me
in the presence of my enemies;
you anoint my head with oil;
my cup overflows.
Surely goodness and mercy shall follow me all the days of my life,
and I shall dwell in the house of the Lord my whole life long.

7. Write a paraphrase of this psalm in your own words. You may uncover some of the difficult emotions the writer must have been experiencing, as he struggled through to find faith. Share your thoughts, if you feel comfortable, in pairs.

Reading Scripture and asking questions

The generic questions, adapted for use here are from *Disciple: becoming disciples through Bible study* (Nashville TN, The United Methodist Publishing House). Used by permission. You may want to have a look at them before reading the passage.

Matthew 20:1-16

For the kingdom of heaven is like a landowner who went out early in the morning to hire labourers for his vineyard. After agreeing with the labourers for the usual daily wage, he sent them into his vineyard. When he went out about nine o'clock, he saw others standing idle in the market-place; and he said to them, "You also go into the vineyard, and I will pay you whatever is right." So they went. When he went out again about noon and about three o'clock, he did the same. And about five o'clock he went out and found others standing around; and he said to them, "Why are you standing here idle all day?" They said to him, "Because no one has hired us." He said to them, "You also go into the vineyard."

When evening came, the owner of the vineyard said to his manager, "Call the labourers and give them their pay, beginning with the last and then going to the first." When those hired about five o'clock

7

came, each of them received the usual daily wage. Now when the first came, they thought they would receive more; but each of them also received the usual daily wage. And when they received it, they grumbled against the landowner, saying, "These last worked only one hour, and you have made them equal to us who have borne the burden of the day and the scorching heat." But he replied to one of them, "Friend, I am doing you no wrong; did you not agree with me for the usual daily wage? Take what belongs to you and go; I choose to give to this last the same as I give to you. Am I not allowed to do what I choose with what belongs to me? Or are you envious because I am generous?"

So the last will be first, and the first will be last.

 Individually answer these questions.

8a. What does the passage say about God?

8b. What does the passage say about human beings?

8c. What does the passage say about the relationship between God and human beings?

 Now in groups of three or four, go round one at a time giving

everyone the opportunity to share their thoughts. Respectfully accept each person's answer. When each person has had the opportunity to speak their answer to each of the questions, allow a conversation to emerge.

The Methodist emphasis

How did John Wesley approach the Scriptures?

In the preface to the *Forty-Four Sermons*, first published in 1746, John Wesley wrote:

> I want to know one thing – the way to heaven; how to land safe on that happy shore. God himself has condescended to teach the way; for this very end he came from heaven. He hath written it down in a book. O give me that book! At any price give me the book of God! I have it: here is knowledge enough for me. Let me be homo unius libri [a man of one book] ... In [God's] presence I open, I read his book; for this end, to find the way to heaven. Is there a doubt concerning the meaning of what I read? Does anything appear dark or intricate? I lift up my heart to the Father of Lights ... I then search after and compare parallel passages of Scripture ... I meditate thereon with all the attention and earnestness of which my mind is capable. If any doubt still remains, I

consult those who are experienced in the things of God; and then the writings whereby, being dead, they yet speak. And what I thus learn, that I teach.

9. What do you learn from this quotation about Wesley's view of Scripture and his way of understanding it?

8

a ....

....

....

b ....

....

....

c ....

....

....

9

....

....

....

....

....

....

What does engaging with Scripture mean to you?

 Look at these statements about what the Bible has meant to different people. Which one interests you, grabs your attention and why? Highlight or underline the phrases which have meaning for you.

A village woman in Africa always used to walk around carrying her Bible. "Why always the Bible?" her neighbours asked her. "There are so many other books you can read." The woman knelt down, held the Bible high above her head and said: "Yes, of course there are many books which I could read. But there is only one book which reads me."

Hans-Ruedi Weber, The book that reads me (World Council of Churches publications, 1995) Used by permission

Most people are bothered by those passages of Scripture which they cannot understand. But as for me, I always notice that the passages of Scripture which trouble me most are those that I do understand.

Mark Twain

If you want to keep people subjugated, the last thing you place in their hands is a Bible. There's nothing more radical, nothing more revolutionary, nothing more subversive against injustice and oppression than the Bible.

Archbishop Desmond Tutu

*Christians do not believe **in** the Bible; they believe in the living God attested by the Bible. Scripture is indispensable in bringing us into a new relationship with the living God through Christ by the power of the Holy Spirit, and thus into new relationship with others and with the entire creation. To speak of the authority of the Bible rightly is to speak of its power by God's Spirit to help create and nourish this new life in relationship with God and with others.*

Daniel L Migliore, Faith seeking understanding (William B Eerdmans Publishing Co; second revised edition 2004) Used by permission

 10. What does the Bible mean to you?

Prayer reflection

Within Scripture there are many examples of prayer, not least in the Psalms.

 Each person has a piece of paper and completes the first line – a name for God. Then each person folds the top of the paper down to cover what they have just written, as if playing 'consequences'. Each person passes the

paper on and completes the next line and folds it. This is repeated until all lines are complete. Each person passes it on once more and then unfolds the paper. Now read out the resulting prayers.

A Bible passage to look at this week

(Rather than a Bible passage, here is a way of reading Bible passages.)

Christians speak of the Bible as inspired. They believe that those who collected the stories and wrote them down, and those that may have spoken the words in the first place were inspired by God, the Holy Spirit. In addition God inspires the reader(s) today, speaking through the words written centuries ago (see page 78).

Christians speak of the Bible as having authority. Over many generations and contexts the words have proved to have been an effective means of God revealing God's self to humans.

The Bible is the word of God. Christ is the living Word of God. Individually and together we break open the word (wrestle to understand its meaning) in order that Christ the living Word finds us and speaks into our lives and communities.

Spiritual reading

Spiritual reading is an ancient way of reflectively reading Scripture with your head and your heart. It is a way of speaking your deepest thoughts to God, and learning to listen to what God may be saying to you in and through the text – a way of reading the 'word', to hear God's 'word' to you.

It can bring practical wisdom for dealing with day to day situations, and at times you receive the gift of a deep sense of the presence of God with you and sustaining you.

Spiritual reading is a discipline that you can practise on your own. It is also a very powerful way of growing in the Christian way, when done in a group setting.

10

....

....

....

....

Preparation

- Decide how long you will spend in spiritual reading. It is better to commit yourself to a definite time (eg 30 minutes).
- Prepare the 'sacred' ground where you will pray (place a chair near a favourite window, light a candle, arrange some flowers, maybe play some background music).
- Decide on a Bible passage (eg Isaiah 43:1-3; Isaiah 55:1-3; Mark 2:1-12; Mark 10:46-52; Luke 5:1-11; John 5:1-8).
- Have a pen and paper, or notepad available for any insights. You may also want to write down any distracting thoughts, so that you can forget about them now and attend to them later.

The process of spiritual reading

- **Centre yourself.**

  Sit comfortably. Take some deep breaths. Put aside everything else and concentrate on reading and praying over this passage of Scripture.

- **Say a simple prayer.**

  For example,

  Thank you God for this time spent with you.
  Help me to read your words so that they can speak to my needs
  and the situations I am involved in.
  The particular desire on my heart today is for wisdom to know how to deal with…

- **Read the passage very slowly.**

  If possible read it out loud. You may want to read it a couple of times. As your read, notice any word or phrase that speaks to you or catches your attention. When this happens, let your mind and heart hover over it, and chew it over.

  – What does it make you think of?
  – Do you feel joy, anger, frustration, sadness? Why?
  – Imagine yourself having a conversation with God – talk about your thoughts and feelings.
  – What does God say back to you?
  – How do you respond? Why is it relevant?

  When you feel you have received as much as you can, gently read on until the next word or phrase holds your attention.

- **Contemplative pauses**

  You may find that your thoughts and words begin to stop and you have a sense of wanting to rest in a felt sense of the peace and love of God. If so, receive this blessing until it seems right to move on.

- **Review**

  Look back over the time. What were the key insights? You may want to write them down, and consider whether you will do or be anything differently now. Some people express this through creative writing, a drawing, a letter or poem.

- **Closing prayer**

  *Thank you Lord, for this time with you.
  Help me to listen to the insights I have
  received. Amen.*

Prayer to use this week

*Gracious God,
you have given us Holy Scripture for
our learning,
that we may be transformed into the
likeness of your Son.
Help us to hear your words in the Word,
to hear them, read, mark, learn and
inwardly digest them,
so that we might know in ourselves
and in our communities,
your fullness of life that Jesus was born
and died to share with us. Amen.*

The next session will focus on following
Jesus. If you have something that
symbolises or helps you on the journey
that you are making in your Christian
faith, then please bring it. There will be
an opportunity during the session to
share it with others and talk about what
it means to you.

To think about: more on Methodism and the Bible

Many Christian traditions have at their
core a statement of faith in the shape of
a creed, a catechism or a confession. The
Methodist Church has two documents
expounding, explaining and applying
Scripture: John Wesley's *Forty-four sermons*
and his *Explanatory notes upon the New
Testament*. These suggest to us that
wrestling with Scripture is fundamental to
the Methodist way of being Christian.
For John Wesley the Bible was uniquely
authoritative. Twenty years later, in his
Plain account of Christian perfection,
Wesley looked back to 1729 as the year
when he "began not only to read, but
to study the Bible, as the one, the only
standard of truth, and the only model of
pure religion". The Bible was his primary
source for Christian belief and practice.

The principle purpose of Scripture, for
Wesley, was to guide people in "the way
to heaven". It did this, he believed, by
unfolding God's plan of love and salvation
for the world and by showing Christians
how they were to live.

In order to make sense of the Bible,
Wesley encouraged careful and thoughtful
reading. The preface to the *Forty-four*

sermons (see pages 88-89) speaks of praying for illumination to the 'Father of Lights', of studying the whole Bible rather than a few favourite texts, and of using the wisdom of experienced Christians to explain difficult passages. In other words, Wesley recognised that the Holy Spirit helps us to understand Scripture and that we interpret the Bible best in conversation with other Christians.

It would be possible to use quotations like these (and there are many more in Wesley's writings) to show that Wesley took a very simplistic or naïve view of the Bible, but this would not be fair! When some of his early preachers chafed at his expectation that they would read widely and protested "But I read only the Bible", Wesley's reply was stern: "If you need no book but the Bible, you are got above St Paul."

In his *Explanatory notes,* Wesley made the best contemporary scholarship available to the Methodists in an accessible form. And in his Christian Library (which ran to 30 volumes), Wesley abridged and republished many Christian classics, so that Methodists could learn from the saints and scholars of the past. Wesley valued the heritage of Christian tradition, particularly the early Church and the Reformation. He was sure that Christian truth went hand in hand with the right use

of our reason. And he held that the Holy Spirit confirmed the truth of Scripture in the experience of Christian people.

Wesley urged his people to take the Bible seriously and to work at understanding it. They were to read prayerfully and intelligently, using the best resources available to them. They were to expect the encounter with Scripture to be transformative, not merely informative.

Today, the Methodist Church still produces materials to help people engage with the Bible. These include:

- *A Word in Time* – a daily online Bible study (www.methodist.org.uk/bible)
- *The Methodist Prayer Handbook* – produced annually, it has prayers and readings for each day of the year. Ask your minister to see a copy,

Session 7: Following Jesus

Opening prayer

Wonderful God,
we are amazed at your love for us,
shown to us in Jesus
and sensed through the Spirit.
We wonder how to respond.
Can we trust ourselves to you
to go on a strange, attractive journey
into the unknown?
Help us to make up our minds
to find the right path for each one of us
at this moment.
Hear our prayer. Amen.

Welcome

If you had to explain *Compass* to a friend, what would you say? Is there one question above all others that you want to explore? What is it?

Introduction

In this session we are considering what it might mean to follow Jesus.

 What kind of things do we follow? Fill in the chart below.

 If you were going on a journey – what would you want to take with you?

This course is called *Compass* because the Christian life is a journey, one which needs guides and pointers. Here we think about where we are now on that journey.

What kind of things do we follow?	What does this kind of following demand?
Football team	
Facebook friends	
TV dramas, shows or soaps	
Blogs	
Maps	
Other people	
Other (write these in)	

How would you describe where you are on the journey of faith? Use the symbol you have brought to explain your thoughts.

 Look at the diagram on page 108. Identify which of the jigsaw pieces best describes your journey of faith.

1. Is your journey of faith focused in one area or more than one? Why?

2. Is there one thing you know you are going to need for the future? What is it? Why do you think you will need it?

Journeying with Jesus

In the beginning of his ministry Jesus gathered many people around him who had quite different reactions. They were:

- astounded at his teaching (Matthew 7:28)
- alarmed at his actions – healing on the Sabbath (Luke 6:1-11)
- amazed at his miracles – the man let down through the roof (Mark 2:1-12)
- scandalised by his statements – he claims to forgive sins! (Mark 2:6-11)
- drawn to follow Jesus as disciples, both men (Luke 6:12-16) and women (Luke 8:2-3).

To those who chose to follow him, Jesus does not make it easy. He speaks of the radical cost of discipleship:

> *If any want to become my followers, let them deny themselves and take up their cross daily and follow me.*

Luke 9:23

This is a radical denial of self-interest – it is focused on the worship of God, following Jesus, responding to the Holy Spirit, and seeking to meet the needs of others.

'Taking up your cross' has come to mean many things:

- a problem that meekly I have to suffer – 'it's a cross I have to bear!'
- it can be reduced to being an ornament to wear – 'it looks nice!'
- a way of living to be embraced and celebrated
- a daily discipline.

 Share together what you think the implications are for those who today, 'take up their cross daily and follow [Jesus]'.

 3. What implications are there for you?

1

2

3

The Bible and growth

The parable of the sower

Matthew 13:1-9

That same day Jesus went out of the house and sat beside the lake. Such great crowds gathered around him that he got into a boat and sat there, while the whole crowd stood on the beach. And he told them many things in parables, saying: "Listen! A sower went out to sow. And as he sowed, some seeds fell on the path, and the birds came and ate them up. Other seeds fell on rocky ground, where they did not have much soil, and they sprang up quickly, since they had no depth of soil. But when the sun rose, they were scorched; and since they had no root, they withered away. Other seeds fell among thorns, and the thorns grew up and choked them. Other seeds fell on good soil and brought forth grain, some a hundred-fold, some sixty, some thirty. Let anyone with ears listen!"

Growth

In twos or threes, consider the parable of the sower. There are different ways of looking at this parable but one is to think of the responses people can have to the message of God's grace in Jesus Christ.

4. As you read this parable, how would you describe the way the responses might happen today?

5. How would you describe the factors for you that could be described as 'good soil'?

Matthew 13:18-23

Hear then the parable of the sower. When anyone hears the word of the kingdom and does not understand it, the evil one comes and snatches away what is sown in the heart; this is what was sown on the path. As for what was sown on rocky ground, this is the one who hears the word and immediately receives it with joy; yet such a person has no root, but endures only for a while, and when trouble or persecution arises on account of the word, that person immediately falls away. As for what was sown among thorns, this is the one who hears the word, but the cares of the world and the lure of wealth choke the word, and it yields nothing. But as for what was sown on good soil, this is the one who hears the word and understands it, who indeed bears fruit and yields, in one case a hundredfold, in another sixty, and in another thirty.

Obstacles to growth

6. What do you think are the things that would hinder your growth as a Christian?

4

5

6

7a. What are the 'birds that steal', 'the scorching sun' and 'the rocky ground' in your life that prevent growth?

7b. What are the 'thorns'?

7c. How can we prevent shallow soil?

Types of growth

John Wesley identified two themes that he thought were vital for the people called Methodists (for more information, see page 106).

- **acts of piety** – prayer, Bible study, fellowship, conferring together, receiving Holy Communion (ie inward practices)
- **acts of mercy** – visiting prisons, caring for the poor, standing up for justice and seeking peace (ie outward practices).

Both were important.

 8. How do the things you have identified earlier about growth (pages 94-95) fit with these two aspects of discipleship which John Wesley urged on the Methodists of his day?

9. Would you want to amend or add to acts of piety and mercy? If so, how?

10. How would you describe them today?

The Methodist emphasis

The Methodist Church as a discipleship movement shaped for mission

To be a disciple of Jesus today involves the whole of our lives. Following Jesus affects the way we view the world and how we live in it, whether at home, at work, with neighbours, friends or strangers. There should be no distinction between our life at church and elsewhere. It is, however, a lifelong commitment. Because we are human we are bound to get it wrong at times. Thankfully God is loving and forgiving and helps us, by the Holy Spirit, to learn from our mistakes and develop.

Martyn Atkins, as General Secretary of the Methodist Church, put it this way:

Methodist Christian discipleship is
rooted and focused on Jesus Christ,
resourced by the Spirit of God,
is both lifelong and whole-life,
communal rather than solitary,
committed to transforming and serving
'the world',
locally, nationally and globally
and so is lived out on a 'big map',
all offered as worship to God as loving
obedience.

Discipleship ... and the people called Methodists (Peterborough, Methodist Publishing, 2010) p.1

7

a ....
....

b ....
....

c ....
....

8

....
....
....

9

acts of piety	acts of mercy

10

acts of piety	acts of mercy

Our Calling

The Methodist Church agreed themes under the title *Our Calling* at the Conference in 2000. There are four main themes intended to describe the work of the Methodist Church (see page 101).

 11a. In worship we experience friends and strangers, words, music, bread and wine. When, for you, does worship move to be an experience of awe and wonder, challenge and transformation?

11b. What has helped you deepen your faith in God, and how do you see pastoral care being offered?

11c. How has the church, in your experience, been a good neighbour to those in need? In what ways has injustice been challenged?

11d. What do you think are appropriate ways of sharing the faith in your community, and nurturing new Christians in the faith?

My calling

 12. Spend a little time quietly thinking about the way God is prompting you to be involved in the life of the church and the community. Reflect on these questions, and write down your thoughts in the box on page 100.

- *What can I do this week, this month to fulfil part of Our Calling?*
- *What contribution can I make to the life of the church?*
- *Given my experience of God and life, what can I offer in God's name?*
- *Do I need to change some of my priorities to be able to fulfil what seems to be My Calling?*
- *What is God laying on my heart to do, to start, or to be involved with?*
- *What are the needs in our community which we can begin to meet, to make a difference?*

When you are ready share with others.

 Are there ways in which you could, with others, take part in supporting one of the areas? If so, what are they?

Prayer reflection: response and commitment

Following Jesus involves responding to the message of good news, and being committed as a disciple. Some questions to consider include:

- Is this a commitment I wish to make?
- What am I going to do?
- What are the resources I need to be able to grow as a Christian?

11

a ....

....

....

....

....

b ....

....

....

....

c ....

....

....

....

d ....

....

....

....

In these prayers, there is time to reflect on your commitment, and an opportunity to think about the next steps you want to make in faith.

Are you ready to become a member of the Methodist Church as a sign of your commitment to Christ and your determination to live that out in the world?

There will be time to light a candle and place it near the cross, and offer a silent prayer of commitment as you do so, as a sign of your desire to go on journeying with Jesus.

You could use the Covenant Prayer (see page 102).

You may also wish to place one of your shoes near the cross as a sign of your desire to go on journeying with Jesus.

A prayer to use:

Jesus, open my eyes to your presence,
open my ears to your call,
open my heart to your love.
Grant me grace to follow you,
wisdom to discern the way
and strength in times of challenge.
Help me to trust you
and give myself to you,
so that I may follow in your ways
and be your true disciple. Amen.

A Bible passage to look at this week

Then [Jesus] said to them all, "If any want to become my followers, let them deny themselves and take up their cross daily and follow me. For those who want to save their life will lose it, and those who lose their life for my sake will save it. What does it profit them if they gain the whole world, but lose or forfeit themselves?"

Luke 9:23-25

12	Worship		Learning & caring
	Service		Evangelism

Our Calling

The calling of the Methodist Church is to respond to the gospel of God's love in Christ and to live out its discipleship in worship and mission. It does this through:

WORSHIP

The Church exists to increase awareness of God's presence and to celebrate God's love.

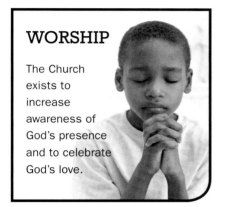

LEARNING & CARING

The Church exists to help people to grow and learn as Christians, through mutual support and care.

SERVICE

The Church exists to be a good neighbour to people in need and to challenge injustice.

EVANGELISM

The Church exists to make more followers of Jesus Christ.

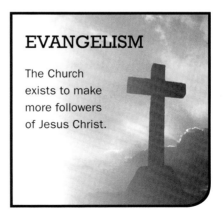

Prayer to use this week

This is a version of the Covenant Prayer, from the Methodist Covenant Service.

I am no longer my own but yours.
Your will, not mine, be done in all things,
wherever you may place me,
in all that I do
and in all that I may endure;
when there is work for me
and when there is none;
when I am troubled
and when I am at peace.
Your will be done
when I am valued
and when I am disregarded;
when I find fulfilment
and when it is lacking;
when I have all things,
and when I have nothing.
I willingly offer
all I have and am
to serve you,
as and where you choose.

Glorious and blessèd God,
Father, Son and Holy Spirit,
you are mine and I am yours.
May it be so for ever.
Let this covenant now made on earth
be fulfilled in heaven. Amen.

Methodist Worship Book, pp. 288-289

To think about: symbols of discipleship

The early Church had many symbols to indicate they were followers of Jesus. This was important when Christianity was outlawed by the state and Christians were imprisoned and tortured. They developed a simple sign using the Greek word for fish: Ἰχθυς and made it into an important statement by using each letter to start a word:

ΙΧΘΥΣ
Ιησους
Χριστος
Θεου
‘**Υ**ιος
Σωτερ

(pronounced 'Yesous Christos Theou Huios Sōter' meaning 'Jesus Christ, of God, Son, Saviour')

 Look around in your church and see if there are Christian symbols woven into the design of the church and its furniture.

13. What does the furniture of the sanctuary (eg pulpit, font, table, Bible) tell you?

14. What other symbols or phrases would you like to see adopted by the Church?

Developing your spiritual life

All of us are on a journey. None of us have arrived, even if we have been on this journey for some time. The spiritual life needs to be nurtured and developed. One of the most important ways to do this is through prayer.

Most people are learners at prayer, and we feel bad because we assume everyone else is an expert. However, prayer itself is a journey, an adventure and a mystery. Get a prayer handbook or some prayers in a style you like and use one a day.

Remember though that prayer is not predominantly about what is said, nor about a place and setting, though they are not unimportant. It is primarily about the joy and mystery of being intentionally in God's presence. Prayer is not learned as one would learn a task like driving a car – gain this skill, pass the test and you can do it. Prayer is more like a relationship, more like being with a dear friend, delighting to be in the presence of the one you care for. That is why reading the Bible is a good way to pray. God speaks as we read the Bible.

Describing prayer as a relationship
There are traditional ways of describing prayer but here is another way of thinking

13

14

about it. If the focus of our understanding of prayer is about a relationship with God then those aspects can be described in this way:

- **wonder** – at the awesome personality of God, God's love and grace, God's greatness and life – we call it *adoration*
- **being grateful** for all God has done for us and others – we call it *thanksgiving*
- **being ashamed** of the things we have done, thought or said or indeed the things we have avoided – we call it *confession* or *penitence*
- **being with others** on our heart – we call it *petition* or *intercession*.

The curious thing about prayer is that we do not really need to tell God anything. God knows already. However like friends who share their deepest feelings, when we give voice to our prayers it strengthens the relationship and accelerates change. The very act of sharing moves people closer. In God's presence, as we share the burdens of our heart and as we hold the people for whom we pray, we move closer to God. Inevitably our lives change: our attitudes, our prejudices, our desires, our values are transformed by his grace.

In prayer and reading the Bible we are:
- re-energised by Christ's presence
- cleansed by his purity
- strengthened by his power
- guided by his word

- assured that he is with others and with us.

15. Write a short prayer using your words and phrases, to express one aspect of prayer.

The Beatitudes

Here is a passage giving guidance about living the Jesus way.

Matthew 5:1-12

When Jesus saw the crowds, he went up the mountain; and after he sat down, his disciples came to him. Then he began to speak, and taught them, saying:

"Blessed are the poor in spirit, for theirs is the kingdom of heaven.
Blessed are those who mourn, for they will be comforted.
Blessed are the meek, for they will inherit the earth.
Blessed are those who hunger and thirst for righteousness, for they will be filled.
Blessed are the merciful, for they will receive mercy.
Blessed are the pure in heart, for they will see God.
Blessed are the peacemakers, for they will be called children of God.
Blessed are those who are persecuted for righteousness' sake, for theirs is the

kingdom of heaven.
Blessed are you when people revile you and persecute you and utter all kinds of evil against you falsely on my account. Rejoice and be glad, for your reward is great in heaven, for in the same way they persecuted the prophets who were before you."

The Beatitudes (or 'beautiful attitudes') contain both values for living and promises of blessing. They are key characteristics of those who seek to embrace God's kingdom. These are values that Jesus not only talked about and challenged others to live by, but also lived out himself whilst on earth. Whilst many thought (and still think)

that living God's way was about what you knew, Jesus came to show us that it's more about what you do and how you live. Living God's way would bring about a joy ("Blessed ...") that no person or circumstance could take away.

The Beatitudes encourage and challenge disciples of Jesus to live openly (verses 3-4), purposefully (verses 5-6), lovingly (verses 7-8) and differently (verses 9-10). Verses 11-12 remind Jesus' followers that there is a cost too.

 16. Are these still 'beautiful attitudes' in the world today? Do you think they need updating in any way? If so, how?

15

16

Discipleship as whole-life, lifelong & world transforming

The Methodist movement began with small groups exploring what it meant to be disciples of Jesus. In the late 1720s a group of student friends at Oxford University began to meet regularly, first to study together, then to pray, read the Scriptures and attend church. This 'methodical' behaviour attracted attention, and won them a string of mocking nicknames. One of these stuck, and they accepted the label 'Methodists'.

From its eighteenth-century roots Methodism has brought particular emphases (and methods) to its understanding of discipleship.

One Methodist emphasis has been to hold together spiritual discipline (what John Wesley called 'works of piety' such as prayer and worship) with deeds of compassion (what Wesley called 'works of mercy' such as visiting those in prison, caring for the needy, offering education, campaigning against slavery). All of this Wesley thought of as 'means of grace' or in our language 'whole-life discipleship'.

The early Oxford Methodists were committed to prayer, Bible study and public worship, but also spent time visiting people in prison and teaching poor children to read. Wesley's preaching houses in London, Bristol and Newcastle included dispensaries where the poor could receive medical help free of charge, and the Methodists were organised to look after the lonely, the bereaved and those who had fallen on hard times. Methodists were challenged to apply their faith 24/7 – to their relationships, in their homes, in their businesses and in their politics.

Methodist discipleship was, unsurprisingly, methodical. Wesley summed up his guidance for the movement in sets of rules, like the *Rules of the society of the people called Methodists*, published in 1743. These said that the Methodist movement was open to anyone who would commit themselves to three simple principles:

> *Do no harm.*
> *Do good.*
> *Love God.*

Our world may be dubious about rules, but the point behind Wesley's principles was clarifying commitment: Wesley was intentional about forming people as disciples of Jesus.

Small groups were part of Methodism from the very beginning. As the movement spread, local 'societies' (churches) multiplied. As societies grew, they were subdivided into 'classes' of 12 people, each with a leader. The classes met every week, and in the meetings members spoke about what God was doing in their lives. They also faced searching questions about their daily walk with God. The questions covered areas such as sins committed and growth in holiness that week. Belonging to a class and attending the weekly meeting was an essential part of being a Methodist. Methodist discipleship was life-changing and world-transforming. It gave people an assurance of God's love for them. It brought them into a community of faith.

It gave them purpose and direction. And the Methodist movement, at its best, helped Christians to show practical compassion to the needy and to address issues of social injustice (like the transatlantic slave trade). Methodists were committed to applying their faith in daily life and to making a difference in the world.

 Reflect on the three simple principles:

Do no harm.
Do good.
Love God.

How can you live these out during the next week?

Your journey with Jesus

Here are ways in which people speak of their faith journey.

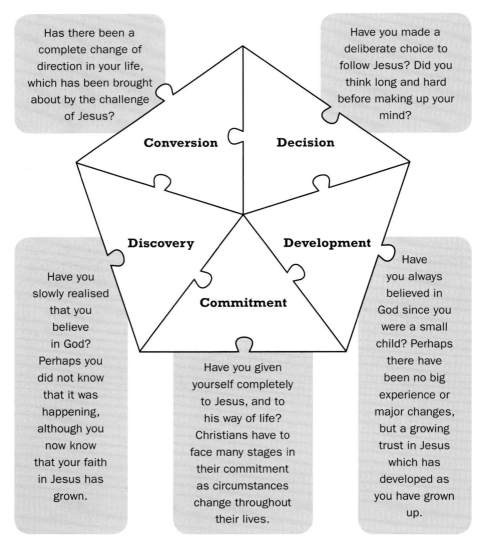

Has there been a complete change of direction in your life, which has been brought about by the challenge of Jesus?

Have you made a deliberate choice to follow Jesus? Did you think long and hard before making up your mind?

Conversion

Decision

Discovery

Development

Commitment

Have you slowly realised that you believe in God? Perhaps you did not know that it was happening, although you now know that your faith in Jesus has grown.

Have you given yourself completely to Jesus, and to his way of life? Christians have to face many stages in their commitment as circumstances change throughout their lives.

Have you always believed in God since you were a small child? Perhaps there have been no big experience or major changes, but a growing trust in Jesus which has developed as you have grown up.

Session 8: Called by name

Opening prayer

Gracious God,
in Jesus and through the Holy Spirit
we have discovered much about you.
We want to respond wholeheartedly to
your love, and share that love with others.
We have heard you call us by name and
dare to say, "Here I am – send me!"
Help us live justly,
be hospitable to friend and stranger,
and courageously risk ourselves in love.
May your peace flow through us to others,
and each day inwardly renew us
through your transforming grace.
Hear our prayer. Amen.

Welcome

Being a Christian involves responding to a sense that God has called us personally and by name to live out a different way of being human in community. This community (the Church) is rooted in God's love and its radical purpose is to be there for those outside itself. This globally-stretching and yet locally-located church community has a rhythm of gathering together in God's name, and mingling in the world to share that love.

 EITHER Read the song "Will you come and follow me?" from the Iona Community about God's call (see page 111).

1a. Which phrase attracts you most, which phrase scares you and which phrase raises a question for you? Think about the reasons for your reactions.

1b. How important is it for you to be called by name? Share your thoughts in threes.

1

a ....

....

b ....

....

OR Look at Roy de Maistre's "The supper at Emmaus" from the Methodist Modern Art Collection (page 118) – Luke 24:13-35.

2. Have there been particular moments when you recognised God's call, where in some way your heart burned within you? Describe one of these moments if you can, or the build up of the feeling.

Membership of the Methodist Church

A [Methodist] society is no other than a company of persons having the form and seeking the power of godliness, united in order to pray together, to receive the word of exhortation, and to watch over one another in love that they may help each other to work out their salvation. John Wesley

The Methodist Church is a huge, worldwide community numbering 80 million. It is part of the universal Church of Christ. But you can't be a Methodist member without belonging to a local Methodist church, and originally 'membership' for the people called Methodists was membership of a small group or class. It was in the class meeting (of 12 or so people) or band (of 4 or 5) that Methodists helped each other discover their gifts, shortcomings and ministries.

The true nature of discipleship is expressed in the Covenant Prayer, the desire to follow Christ in the good times and the bad – this is Methodist's special gift to the worldwide Church. (You will have come across it in Session 7 page 102 as you were invited to use it as the prayer for the week.)

Methodists recall their decision to follow Jesus and renew their commitment in the annual Covenant Service. A covenant is a solemn vow which two parties make to be committed to one another through thick and thin.

2

Will you come and follow me
if I but call your name?
Will you go where you don't know
and never be the same?
Will you let my love be shown,
will you let my name be known,
will you let my life be grown
in you and you in me?

Will you leave yourself behind
if I but call your name?
Will you care for cruel and kind
and never be the same?
Will you risk the hostile stare
should your life attract or scare?
Will you let me answer prayer
in you and you in me?

Will you let the blinded see
if I but call your name?
Will you see the prisoners free
and never be the same?
Will you kiss the leper clean,
and do such as this unseen,
and admit to what I mean in you
and you in me?

Will you love the 'you' you hide
if I but call your name?
Will you quell the fear inside
and never be the same?
Will you use the faith you've found
to reshape the world around,
through my sight and touch and sound
in you and you in me?

Lord, your summons echoes true
when you but call my name.
Let me turn and follow you
and never be the same.
In your company I'll go
where your love and footsteps show.
Thus I'll move and live and grow
in you and you in me.

Words: John L Bell, Graham Maule
© 1987, Wild Goose Resource Group,
Iona Community, Glasgow G2 3DH.
www.wgrg.co.uk. Used by permission.

I am no longer my own but yours.
Your will, not mine, be done in all things,
  wherever you may place me,
  in all that I do
    and in all that I may endure;
  when there is work for me
    and when there is none;
  when I am troubled
    and when I am at peace.
Your will be done
  when I am valued
    and when I am disregarded;
  when I find fulfilment
    and when it is lacking;
  when I have all things,
    and when I have nothing.
I willingly offer
all I have and am
  to serve you,
  as and where you choose.
Glorious and blessèd God,
Father, Son and Holy Spirit,
  you are mine and I am yours.
  May it be so for ever.
  Let this covenant now made on earth
  be fulfilled in heaven. Amen.

Methodist Worship Book, pp. 288-289

 3a. In what ways is it helpful to think of membership of the Methodist Church in terms of a covenant relationship, that involves a whole community and God?

3b. What would be lost if membership was thought of as a short-term agreement or contract?

3c. Why do you think being part of a community with other people is important?

 Share your thoughts with others.

Service of Confirmation and Reception into Membership

The service of Confirmation and Reception into Membership flows on from sacrament of Baptism. In Baptism, God receives us in love unconditionally, before we make any response or commitment. When a baby is baptized, the baby is received before they have any conscious knowledge of God. Following the Baptism, parents make promises to bring their child up with a Christian upbringing. At a later point the grown infant may come to the point of wishing to affirm the parental promises of faith for themselves. In a service of Confirmation they do this, request confirmation of God's continuing gifts of grace that was given to them in their Baptism and are then received into membership of the Methodist Church.

In adult Baptism, the person seeking Baptism may recognise that God has been working in their lives for some time, and that Baptism expresses the sense of the believer realising this and acting upon it. In the same service the person who has just been baptized will seek confirmation of the graces given in Baptism and will be received into full membership of the Church. A service of Confirmation should include the celebration of Holy Communion, to remind us of the 'food' that God provides for our journey of discipleship.

The water used in Baptism powerfully reminds us of stories in the Bible.

- **New creation** (Genesis 1)
  The Spirit of God moved over the waters of chaos when the world and humans were created at the beginning of time. As a new creation, we are reconnected with our true identity as a child of God.

- **Freedom** (Exodus 14:21-22)
  God's people escaped from slavery through the waters which were mysteriously parted. Baptism is a life in the freedom of God's Holy Spirit.

- **New birth** (John 3:3-6)
  No baby is born without the breaking of the waters of the womb, and Baptism

3

a ....

....

....

b ....

....

....

c ....

....

....

is a new birth into a new way of being human.

- **Life** (John 4:7-15)
Jesus tells a woman at the well that he himself is living water, able to quench our deep thirst.

- **Renewal** (John 13:3-15)
Jesus washed the feet of his disciples, symbolically cleansing them and calling them to use their gifts to serve others in the same way.

- **Death and resurrection** (Romans 6:1-4)
Jesus passed through the deep waters of death for our sake, and in Baptism we are symbolically 'buried' and raised to new life through his death and life in us.

 4. Which image of Baptism speaks most to you at this point in your journey of faith?

Service of confirmation
The Service of Confirmation and Reception into Membership can be found in the *Methodist Worship Book,* pp. 97-102.

The affirmation of faith
Do you turn away from evil and all that denies God?
By the grace of God, I do.

Do you turn to God, trusting in Jesus Christ as Lord and Saviour, and the Holy Spirit as Helper and Guide?
By the grace of God, I do.

Methodist Worship Book, pp. 98-99

 5a. What does it mean for you personally to turn away from evil and all that denies God?

5b. What does trusting in Jesus as Saviour and the Holy Spirit as helper mean to you?

The creed
A creed is a summary statement of the tradition of the Church, which has been handed down to us from our ancestors in the faith. It provides a framework for our belief.

In this version (*The Methodist Worship Book, p. 99*) it is framed as a series of questions and responses.

The Confirmation
In the worship service (liturgy) the candidates are confirmed by the Holy Spirit before they make their promises. This is because the power for our new life depends on God, and not on us. We respond to the power that is already given to us.

The minister lays hands on the candidate, in the presence of the assembled congregation, ritually enacting the offering of the God's gift of grace. This is a moment of the public declaration of faith of the candidate, and commitment to be in covenant relationship with this local community, as part of the Church universal. It is also the public declaration of the assembled community, to receive a new member of the community and to be in covenant relationship with this new member. They make promises accordingly.

The promises of those newly-confirmed

Will you commit yourself to the Christian life of worship and service, and be open to the renewing power of God?
With God's help I will.
Will you seek the strength of God's Spirit as you accept the cost of following Jesus Christ in your daily life?
With God's help I will.
Will you witness, by word and deed, to the good news of God in Christ, and so bring glory to God?
With God's help I will.

Methodist Worship Book, pp.100-101

4

5

a

b

6. In what ways would you seek to fulfil these promises?

The promise of the people

After the person being confirmed has made their promises, the minister says to the people:

> *Will you so maintain the Church's life of worship and service that they may grow in grace and in the knowledge and love of God and of his Son Jesus Christ our Lord?*
> **With God's help we will.**

Methodist Worship Book, p.101

7. What do you think you need from the local church community?

8. As a final celebration of everything that you have discovered during this course, use the structure of Psalm 23 to write a prayer of thanksgiving (using your own language, words and imagery) about everything that God means to you.

Psalm 23

The Lord is my shepherd, I shall not want.
He makes me lie down in green pastures;
he leads me beside still waters;
he restores my soul.
He leads me in right paths
for his name's sake.

Even though I walk through the darkest valley,
I fear no evil;
for you are with me;
your rod and your staff—
they comfort me.
You prepare a table before me
in the presence of my enemies;
you anoint my head with oil;
my cup overflows.
Surely goodness and mercy shall follow me
all the days of my life,
and I shall dwell in the house of the Lord
my whole life long.

Prayer reflection

Offer a prayer of thanksgiving for each member of the group, for the richness of the time together, and for everything that people have learnt.

Then close by saying this prayer from the Service of Confirmation and Reception into Membership:

Generous God,
touch us again
with the fire of your Spirit
and renew us by your grace,
that we may profess the one true faith
and live in love and unity
with all who follow Christ. Amen.

Methodist Worship Book, p. 101

6

7

8

The painting shows the moment during the story of the walk to Emmaus (Luke 24:13-35) when the two disciples suddenly recognise the risen Jesus as he breaks bread with them. They say to one another, "Were not our hearts burning within us while he was talking to us on the road, while he was opening the scriptures to us?" (Luke 24:32)